following whispers

ALSO BY DAN THOMPSON

American, Interrupted:
A Soldier's Journal of Operation Iraqi Freedom
from Spring 2003 until Summer 2004

Away with the Gatekeepers:
Social Media as a Tool Facilitating Nonviolent Struggle
During the 2011 Egyptian Revolution

DAN THOMPSON

following
whispers

walking on the rooftop of the world
in nepal's himalayas

DAN THOMPSON BOOKS

Boston • Charleston • Frankfurt • Kathmandu • London • Seoul

www.facebook.com/followingwhispers

ISBN-13: 978-1481026352   ISBN-10: 1481026356
Library of Congress Control Number: 2012921998

Header text is set in Ananda Namaste
Designed by Ananda K. Maharjan of Kathmandu, Nepal © 2011
www.anandakm.com.np

Body text is set in Garamond

First U.S. edition

Printed in the United States of America
Keep America Creative

Inspired in Nepal

For my wife & sons

Nora, Luis, and Liam

He who has done his best for his own time

has lived for all times

⋙ Johann Friedrich Von Schiller ⋘

In memory of Liam Munroe Thompson

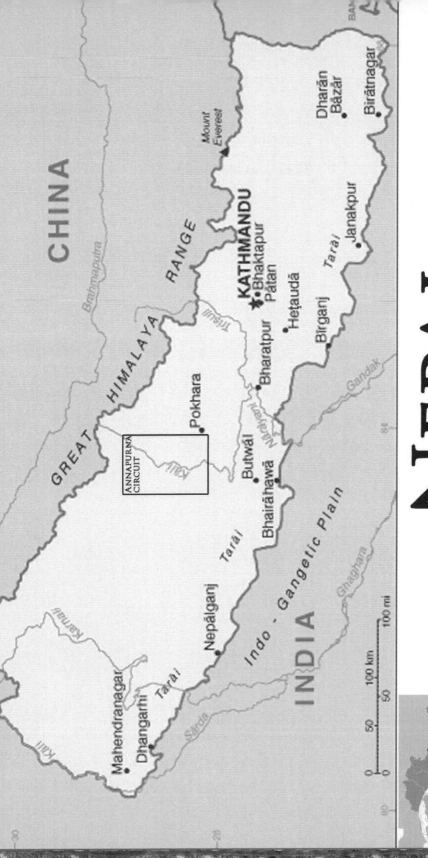

This book is born of chance and the goodwill of strangers scattered across the globe. My own journey to Nepal actually began years before I knew it, when a lady named Priscilla Schwartz and her husband Barry decided to host two young men from Germany and Nepal. The fellow from Germany is my father-in-law, Volker, and the Nepali gentleman is Krishna. As fate would have it, these four people helped make our visit to Nepal possible. But perhaps it wasn't chance or fate at all. What brought these people together was openness to other people, a tradition of hospitality, and perhaps a belief that despite our nationalities, we are more alike than we are different. Whatever the reasons may be, they all made a conscious effort to bring people together in cultural exchange. That alone is hard, time consuming work. It's a selfless labor of love. It's something chance alone cannot accomplish.

And that is where this story really begins. These special people opened a door to Nepal and introduced us to yet another group of hospitable and selfless people who truly made my wife's and my journey there possible. To Krishna's wife Triza, who made us feel at home with her home cooking and care; to Jenash for taking time from his busy schedule as an apprentice medical doctor to introduce us to Kathmandu; and countless other Nepalese who made us feel at home while in their beautiful country. When we needed assistance, they jumped up to help. When we sought medicine, they would scour the markets for us. Despite my wife and I coming from the relatively wealthy West, many would treat us to a meal or drinks, and wave off a series of my pleas that I pay. In the mountains, friendly innkeepers and the superhuman porters who sustained an entire region literally on their backs made our entire journey possible. While Nepal is known for Mount Everest and beautiful vistas, what is truly beautiful are not the mountains, but the warmth of these hospitable people.

Most of all, our journey to Nepal could not have happened without the assistance and selfless hospitality of two very special people, Paras Shrestha and Niraj Tamrakar. These two young men set aside their day jobs for two weeks to walk us every step of the way in the Himalayas. Their patience, kindness, and sense of civic duty humbled and inspired us. Nora and I owe the success of our Annapurna trek to them. More importantly, the wisdom they shared with us broadened our worldview and made us hopeful not only for a more prosperous Nepal, but a hopeful future among our globalized generation.

Were it not for the openness of these people, this journey would not have happened. Their example is a reminder that many people we meet are not anonymous faces, but friends waiting to be made. Each brush with a stranger, be they in our community or a faraway land, is a story waiting to be told. It is one waiting to be written. Nora and I owe this journey to all of those who have revealed this truth to us and renewed its promise wherever we go.

Thank you.

A portion of the sales of this book will go towards supporting sustainable tourism in Nepal.

contents

Preface

I shouldn't have been there, and I knew it. Signs on the barbed wire fence I crawled under to get there forbid entry, taking photos, or drawing any maps of the area – by order of a Navy base commander. As I stood at the mouth of a huge storm water pipe like a cave in the forest, I had a decision to make. Should I turn around now or commit to push deeper into the snake-infested marshland? Was it worth getting in trouble to find out what mysteries waited to be uncovered at Charleston Naval Weapons Station, South Carolina? To prove to myself that I could go where no other ten-year-old Navy brat had been before?

The answer was *yes*. The temptation to discover every detail of the forest was irresistible, like a magnet to metal. Stepping across a stream of sewage littered with rusted bikes, I crossed from the known into the unknown. I knew it was dangerous. I knew my backside would pay for it once my parents found out, but it didn't matter to me. Pushing deeper into the woods, I found signs of life – a camp built out of scrap metal and tarps, rusted hulks of old military gear and waterlogged *Playboy* magazines. While I could very well have stumbled into some kind of homicidal hobo camp, it was fascinating in more ways than one. I continued on until finding the edge of a marsh and beautiful tributary of the Cooper River. Like floating logs, I could spot alligator heads sitting perfectly still on the calm waters, their barking calls echoing through the forest.

My journey ended about a mile away from where it began, but not before discovering a mysterious barrel. In my imagination, it was some kind of nuclear waste. When my distraught parents finally tracked me down, when I reemerged from the barbed wire hours later, I tried in vain to convince them of my expedition's success. I discovered toxic waste, and if it weren't for my trek, it would continue to pollute the area. My dad called in my discovery to the authorities, but it didn't change the fact that I was grounded for life. But I was newly inspired, covering distances on foot that I thought in my young mind were only possible by car. I came within rock throwing distance of alligators, copperheads, and sunning rat snakes. I escaped capture by hobos! Discovered toxic waste! All of the highlights that made my journey so exciting were also what made parents and military base commanders freak out. Hence, the barbed wire.

To me, that fence was oppressive. It kept me *out* and its secrets *in*. It was there to be defeated, I thought. Exploring the woods wasn't bad. I did it, and did it successfully. I lived to tell the story. I listened to that whispering of the adventurous heart that prods one faster, further, and longer. The secret was out from that day on. I had to follow my heart and overcome obstacles. I had to follow those whispers. It was then that my wanderlust was born.

Around the same time, I remember reading about Nepal. I was sitting on the floor of my bedroom in Navy housing pouring over a copy of *National Geographic Magazine*. The issue featured a story about the excruciating climb up Mount Everest, and depicted a trail map outlining the summit. I traced a line with my finger from Everest Base Camp up to Camp IV, and then on to the summit at 28,029 feet. I understood that was very high, but didn't realize at the time that it could kill you. I read about sherpas routinely carrying gear up the mountain like mystical supermen with Mongolian faces. I imagined the Himalayas as a majestic land blanketed in a purple hue of eternal dusk with stars shining across the sky like diamonds. I imagined Nepal to be no larger than a small American town, with people dressed in scarlet robes passing the time away.

I also remember wanting to go there, but it seemed impossible. It seemed so remote. Somewhere deep inside, though, I remember telling myself that I would make it there. The distance and details of getting there were like the barbed wire fence my backside was smacked for crossing: it could be overcome. Uncharted territory was nothing to be afraid of, I thought. It was like a puzzle waiting to be assembled into a clear picture. Sure, there may be alligators and snakes out there, and strange looking women in magazines, but nothing that a little preparation and caution couldn't handle. From that moment on, I realized there was the world of free-ranging gators, and then there was *Gatorland*. There were hobo camps and then there was *COPS* on TV. There was the real world waiting to be experienced, touched, and tasted – or, there was a safer caricature one could vicariously live the real world through using TV and amusement parks. I was hooked on the real world, where risk was rewarded with vivid memories, great tales to tell, and a sense of accomplishment. I blame *National Geographic Magazine*.

That sense of adventure guided a large part of my life. It later carried me, and my wife Nora, around the world from Boston to Bali and Macau to Morocco. With my military service in Iraq from 2003-2004 as a U.S. Army soldier, my sense of adventure meshed with my new curiosity about other cultures, especially in the East. For me, the East was like that forbidden pine forest of my childhood. I'd never been there, never touched it, never explored it. That would all change when we met Krishna.

Nora and I first met Krishna at her parents' home in Frankfurt, Germany in 2004. A man in his fifties, Krishna ran a non-governmental organization in Nepal for the disabled, and occasionally made the journey west to meet with old friends and international exchange organizations. He and Nora's father were introduced to each other through a family friend, philanthropist and world traveler, Priscilla Schwartz. All of them were bound together by a love of international exchange and culture. Krishna's friendly demeanor was unmistakable, his laugh always genuine, his smile always thoughtfully gauged and his questions refreshingly frank at times. I liked him almost immediately, and when he cooked a traditional Nepali dinner for us all one night, he might as well have stolen my curry-loving heart. The truth was, since returning from Iraq, I missed oriental peoples. He suggested several times that we visit Nepal, telling us about its beauty, and how much easier it would be to see the country with local contacts like him. It was a convincing pitch. I thought back to those early ideas about Nepal as a child and thought, *why not?* One evening, I promised Krishna that we would visit him in Nepal – and I fully intended to visit sooner rather than later.

So, what is it about the East that draws some westerners? It is a question that obviously has many answers, but one need only look to western pop culture to find a few. From the Beatles to Madonna, many western prophets of pop have sought to escape the spiritual void of the West for more exotic locations like India and Nepal. The Beatles made their journey to India in 1968 to awaken their inner selves at an ashram, pursue the art of meditation, adopt a vegetarian diet and learn yoga. Even the *Fab Four* needed a break from the wild kingdom they had almost single-handedly created.

The hippie gospel of sex, drugs, and rock and roll failed to address the deeper spiritual needs of its followers, and many of them hit the "Hippie Trail" from Istanbul to Nepal to find inner peace through a thick haze of ganja smoke and a technicolor LSD alternative reality. Cat Stevens captured his feelings about this psychedelic "freak" movement in his song "Kathmandu," which he wrote in a Nepali teahouse. The freaks are mostly gone from Kathmandu's streets, which once attracted thousands of pot-smoking hippies during the 60s and early 70s, but unofficial names like "Freak Street" still remain. Now, some aging baby boomer freaks can still be spotted reminiscing on Durbar Square in Kathmandu, not looking very groovy in their khaki shorts, fanny packs, and exhausted facial expressions underneath tufts of graying hair. Now, their children and grandchildren roam the streets of Kathmandu, not in tie-dye shirts but expensive Columbia and North Face garb made in Vietnam and China. Although some of them are there to find ever-elusive inner peace, many are there to indulge in the ganja and find something more adventuresome than the dull western life they left behind. Still, others go to truly become Nepali for a while, to learn something new.

Nora and I had our own reasons for going to Nepal. We wanted to be immersed in its culture, experience something exotic, and get out into the great outdoors to recharge our spirits. In late 2006, after the death of my grandmother, I thought about my grandparents' example. Their stories were, of course, flawed, as many human stories are, but they were also inspiring. A sailor turned draftsman, a runaway turned successful businessman, a small town girl working for the FBI becomes a radio station manager, and a Pennsylvania girl grows up to travel all over the U.S. and Australia. Their paths weren't clear-cut. They didn't follow a linear path to success. They took risks, they adapted, and most of all, they left home to find success. They epitomized the American can-do spirit many associate with better times. They followed the whispers of their own hearts, and they succeeded. As my fingers traced my grandmother's urn one last time at her funeral in 2006, I was reminded that life was short, and like my grandparents, I needed to make the most of my time. When I returned home to Frankfurt in December, I decided we were going to keep that casual promise made to Krishna. We were going to Nepal.

I would rather be ashes than dust!
I would rather that my spark
should burn out in a brilliant blaze
than it should be stifled by dry-rot.

I would rather be a superb meteor,
every atom of me in magnificent glow,
than a sleepy and permanent planet.

The function of man is to live, not to exist.

I shall not waste my days trying to prolong them.

I shall use my time.

≈ Attributed to Jack London ≈

Nepal is not here for you

It is not here for you to change

It is here to change you

≈ Sign at Tribhuvan International Airport ≈

following whispers

the departure

Ever since being sent to Iraq as a U.S. soldier, I considered myself a veteran traveler. In hindsight, I was anything but. Aside from a combat deployment, a vacation to Egypt and Turkey, and some misadventures in Western Europe, most European students traveled more in their gap year than I had in my entire life. Just how inexperienced I was became easier for me to admit as my wife and I planned our trip to Nepal. Of course, we ordered the obligatory *Lonely Planet* guides. But, even after pouring over most of the pages, I was suspicious of references to backpacker bars and black market CD shops in the tourist districts. I was looking for something more. I didn't want to have access to the internet, to western beer or the best spaghetti in Kathmandu. I wanted to experience Nepal like a local. But first, we needed to figure out what to take with us. With a little help from Krishna's son via e-mail, our understanding of Nepal was slowly improving. We knew we would stay a few nights at Krishna's house, but in the mountains we needed gear for both colder elevations and hot conditions at lower altitude. There was something exciting about throwing ourselves headfirst into a part of the world we didn't know. There was an inherent challenge in packing for a wide range of conditions. The sense of adventure was building, but so were the occasional flashes of sober reason: we had no idea what we were getting in to. Perhaps to soothe this uncertainty, we hedged our bets and made sure we were ready for anything.

Those bets would be expensive. To visit some of the poorest places on Earth, we apparently needed some of the priciest outdoor gear from North Face, Columbia, Jack Wolfskin, and so on. I browsed stores with knotted eyebrows while examining a 530 Euro sleeping bag made in China and a breathable jacket made in Bangladesh. There was some irony in spending so much just to take gear almost back to its country of origin, where someone probably made the stuff for a few dollars.

We couldn't avoid buying good gear, but waited until the last minute before we finally gave in and bought some high quality kit. The week before our departure was spent hurriedly shopping for two light but warm sleeping bags that, at Nora's insistence, zipped together to form one large love nest. It later turned out to be a genius idea. Less romantic purchases led to some curious glances from the cashier at the local army store. A large knife, a hefty first aid kit, water purification pumps, water purification tablets, polyester military-issue undershirts, and rehydration salts perhaps seemed like an odd match for their pudgy customer. I imagine they thought I was off to have a heart attack somewhere in the Alps, or was just another plump civilian over-prepared for an upcoming stint in Iraq or Afghanistan. Over-prepared? Perhaps. With the gear we purchased, it was clear that I would be able to turn raw sewage into refreshing mineral water, conduct minor surgery with a comprehensive first aid kit, medicate half the population of Nepal against diarrhea, and hold off a tiger with the large knife. Except for the medical kit, which turned out to be critical, most of what we bought never saw the light of day in Nepal.

In the days leading up to our departure, I joked with work colleagues about not coming home alive from my trip. Many people I talked to thought I was mad for going anywhere east. As far as they were concerned, Nepal bordered Iraq. My mother tried to dissuade me from trekking to my doom and being eaten by Maoist cannibals. In a last-minute attempt to change my mind, she e-mailed several images of angry communist Nepalese burning effigies and screaming. But, unless the Maoists were willing to refund my ticket, I wasn't canceling my plans. The truth was, Nepal had undergone political change for some time, but was finally on the verge of a power-sharing agreement with the subversive Maoist groups. Since 2006, over 10,000 people died in a bloody insurgency – largely unnoticed by the outside world. My mother noticed, though, and understandably protested our trip. After reading her disapproving e-mail, I promptly registered Nora and myself with the U.S. embassy in Kathmandu.

The night before flying to Nepal, Nora and I ran a marathon down Frankfurt's city streets trying to buy gifts for Krishna and his family before the stores closed. It was late in the evening and we both felt the pressure of having procrastinated. But the evening offered a fascinating lesson. We were determined to find gifts made in Germany; an Adidas shirt, a Puma hat, a beer stein, perhaps. We were dumbfounded combing shops to find goods imported from Asia – our destination. We found Adidas and Puma apparel at a sports shop, but a quick look at the tags indicated that they were made in China, which neighbors Nepal. Eventually, we settled for a baseball cap made in China but embroidered with the local Frankfurt soccer team's logo for Krishna's son. Other items included perfume sets made in France, cologne made in Germany, and a nice picture book of Frankfurt. The experience left me wondering, what exactly was typically German anymore?

Our flight was scheduled for the next morning. Anyone who believes in the superior refinement of Europe surely hasn't visited the Frankfurt International Airport. There, a sampling Germany's equivalent of American rednecks, bound for cheap hotels in the *Med* and elsewhere, crowd the halls like cattle. Overweight men with bouffant hair, nutcracker-tight shorts, tanning bed hides and glittering gold necklaces tangled in their exposed chest hair stand with their families waiting to check luggage for their flight to Mallorca. Some walk about apishly with beer bellies prominently leading the way. Their arms dangle lifelessly at their sides. As Nora and I stood in line to check in for our afternoon flight to Doha, Qatar, I chuckled to myself. German efficiency in the form of a line attendant kept a watchful eye out for anyone cutting in, and aggressively chided those who tried. It was one of the few times I was thankful for German bureaucracy.

Suddenly breaking the monotony of the moment, a couple appeared who would accompany us on the flight. They were slim and dressed in all black, tight-fitting North Face adventure gear. The woman, although petite, possessed a frog-like physique with bulging thighs and muscular arms; perfectly built for climbing and trekking. Her companion was lanky, but they shared one thing in common – their demeanor. Perhaps out of giddiness that we were about to leave for Nepal, combined with slight boredom, my imagination came alive. I named the two Europeans Pierre and Brigitte, and they were the perfect living oh-so-Euro caricatures, confidently pouting in line. I imagined them both prancing effortlessly like spring deer up the side of Mount Everest and then both smoking a cigarette – defiantly exhaling smoke – while taking in the view from the top of the world's highest point. I shared my delusions with Nora and we both laughed, moving a few steps closer to the check-in counter.

After receiving our boarding passes, we moved directly to the passport and security checks. Sensing the irritation of a growing herd of confused tourists wandering towards the security checks, I gave Nora a signal, and we quickened our step to pass them. A middle-aged man unashamedly rammed his luggage trolley into a child's stroller to get ahead of the crowd. The uncivilized procession of Europeans became frustrated when, just around the corner they were trying so dishonorably to pass, stood a long line of folks waiting to be screened.

Passing German passport control has always been a tense experience since a frowning immigration officer berated me for possessing a less than perfect passport. Admittedly, the pages were almost full and the lamination had yellowed a bit from the elements, but mine was a traveler's passport – not a tourist one.

"Is this what you call a passport?!" he yelled in German as I was on my way to board a flight to Egypt years ago. He held the passport between his thumb and index finger and shook it violently to see if it would break. I sharply demanded my passport back and told him that I would order a new one as soon as I could. He sneered and tossed it on the countertop. This turned out to be an isolated incident and I was never challenged again, but I always suspected that the *Bundesgrenzschutz* would once again school me on proper passport appearance. This time, as I waited for a Ghanaian woman ahead of me to clear passport control, quite the opposite happened.

"Your passport is expired," said an officer bluntly after thumbing at abnormal length through her passport pages. "Did you know this?"

The woman shook her head and looked somewhat confused, "No, I did not know."

"Look, your passport expired eight days ago," he said. "Are you going home?"

"Yes, I am going back," she replied eagerly.

"I will let you through, but you need to get a new passport when you return."

"Yes, yes," she said relieved. "I will do that." And without further delay, he stamped her passport and allowed her to go on her way. Conceivably, he could have kept her waiting, but he was quite helpful. I was next.

"Good morning," I said in German.

"Morning," he replied. "Are you going to Doha on duty or holiday?" he asked, correctly assuming that I was associated with the military.

"On holiday," I replied. He promptly stamped my passport and accepted my thanks. It shouldn't have surprised me, except for my posttraumatic passport stress, but I was relieved to get past without further interrogation or the *passport maracas* routine.

Frankfurt International Airport has a special place in my heart for good and bad reasons. As we waited to board our flight, Nora and I sat nibbling on some french-fries near a large row of windows offering a panoramic view of the flight line and nearby gates. From where I sat,

I could see gate A15 where, in 2002, some Army buddies and I boarded a flight for a blurred vacation week in London. I looked across the airfield at the radio tower on what used to be Rhein-Main Airbase, where I first set foot in Europe in 1998. I noticed the observation deck where I stood in 2000, brokenhearted, as a girl I once loved took off in a jet bound for Dublin. It was the place where I met my biological father for the first time in memory. It was where Nora and I, madly in love, reunited after meeting in the U.S. in 2001 and decided to live together in Germany. It was the place where I departed for Rome and the Vatican in 2003, just before being sent to the Iraq War, looking for inspiration. I later returned here to a brass band welcoming us home from that 14 month deployment. For many people, Frankfurt Airport was a stopover. For me, it was a center of gravity.

The airline we flew prided itself on being five-star. I tend to agree with them. As we boarded a bus that would carry us to the plane, I remembered the company's ad campaign on CNN portraying the company as the finest airline in the sky. My expectations were not disappointed as we boarded our flight, and a very courteous flight attendant showed us to our seats. The interior was meticulously kept, the staff looked professional, and best of all, economy-class seats had generous leg room. It felt like we were sitting in business class, as if I really knew what that was like. After years of flying on the cheapest seats possible, I felt like a Beverly Hillbilly marveling at the in-flight goodie bag and shared my excitement with Nora in my best hillbilly accent. It was exciting to be going somewhere new, to be going with such a nice airline, and to be going back to Doha after having been there almost exactly three years earlier during the war.

Shortly after takeoff from Frankfurt, we cruised over Munich and Slovenia as the flight attendants passed out menu cards. We received a five-course meal and full drink service. I took some time to watch the airline's promotional video and chuckled as the screen read "The runway is privileged," thinking about the gulf Arab mentality. Privileged status is more important than merit. Their marketing team definitely wanted to convey an image of exclusivity, luxury, and finery.

In a symbolic display of their friendliness towards westerners, drink carts conspicuously displayed several tall bottles of hard liquor, which none of the passengers seemed interested in. In much the way many see Arabs as AK-47-wielding terrorists, they see westerners as raving alcoholics who prefer drinking Smirnoff to water. It's a phenomenon I've encountered in the East before, and I am not quite sure why many believe we all live Las Vegas-style lives full of drugs and fast women. With a long flight ahead, I took some time to write in my journal.

March 16, 2007 9:37 p.m.
West of Jawf, Saudi Arabia at 41,000 feet
It is with absolute pleasure that I find myself making a journey east towards Nepal. There is a certain magic, an energetic pulse, in the Orient from Turkey and beyond. The sun has long set as our flight cruised past Ankara, Turkey and Homs, Syria. I have been listening to the sounds of Arabian violins serenade my ears on the in-flight music channel; piquing my memory of late night dinners [with Iraqi translators] in Baghdad, Iraq – only about an hour's flight from where I hang in the sky now.

I imagine our airliner as a flashing star in the Arabian night – perhaps catching the attention of herders sitting by their bonfires in the middle of the desolate – almost lunar – Saudi desert.

Despite the incredible hardships that I experienced in Iraq, there is something redeeming about returning to the Middle East, and ironically enough, to Doha, Qatar, with Nora by my side. Deep inside, there is a part of me that feels at home in the region and hopeful for its future. But enough waxing philosophic; Nora and I will not be staying in the Middle East, but rather in Nepal – the farthest east we have traveled.

For some reason, the night approach into Doha brought back vivid memories of my deployment to the Middle East in 2003 – the horizon that stretched forever; the oasis of electrical lights in the desert; the strong winds that made our hard landing a hair-raising experience. I faintly felt like I was back for duty. As the young American men with buzz cuts deplaned, I felt a bit of relief and fortune to be a simple traveler with no base to report to. When Nora and I stepped off of the aircraft, the warm gulf night enveloped and greeted me like an old acquaintance. I knew Doha, and admired its deep sapphire blue night sky years ago. It was good to be back.

Doha International Airport was a bustling little place with a stately, glowing white interior with silver accents. Arab customs officers in long, white flowing *jellabahs*[1] and traditional red *smaghs*[2] glided across arrivals hall and expressionlessly stamped passports. We needed to catch a 2 a.m. flight to Kathmandu, and didn't have the $100 visa needed to explore Doha. There was plenty of culture on display in the arrival hall, though. Except for the noticeably large numbers of French and British travelers, it was definitely clear that we were no longer in the west as veiled women and men with long beards walking in sandals greatly outnumbered the westerners.

When we entered the arrival hall, I watched as the X-ray machine operator in a police uniform was pestered by a wildly talkative airport staffer. The policeman looked irritated, and I wasn't quite sure if he could effectively screen the bags. I was reminded that we were back in the sometimes chaotic and abstract Arab world, where one's profession seems subordinate in importance to loose social demands…in this case, lending a sympathetic ear to an annoying coworker.

The departure hall looked like the set of a *Star Wars* bar scene. South Asian and African laborers, Pakistani tribesmen bound for Peshwar, Afghani Pashtuns, Wahabi Saudis, and others all mixed and sat about awaiting their flights, while ignoring the skimpily dressed – and loud – British girls. There was such an eclectic mix of cultures and unlikely neighbors sitting next to each other on lounge chairs – a French woman clutching her purse uncomfortably as a young Arab teen tried to sleep next to her with a newspaper over his head. A fat old

---

[1] Traditional robe. Also known as a *dishdasha* or *thobe*.

[2] Traditional head covering resembling a large scarf. Usually held in place by a ring of black rope called an *igal*.

Arab man sat at a distance from his two young veiled wives while his two young daughters, dressed like Little Debbie, entertained a British couple. A group of Taliban-looking men sat next to a publically affectionate French couple. This was like the Grand Central Station to the East, but with dedicated Muslim prayer rooms.

Our five-star airline lived up to its reputation, until our flight was delayed seven hours. The delay wasn't announced. Rather, the digital screen simply flickered with the new information and the motley crew of Mongolian-faced laborers, western trekkers, and Nepali folks returning home from their second homes abroad took the news with a dignified sigh. There was no rush to the customer service desk for a meal ticket or accommodations. They were second-class citizens in Qatar and would never receive such a perk. While I asked a staff member about accommodations, he dismissed a British-educated Nepali student in the same situation as mine. I was a bit puzzled when the staff member took my passport and returned half an hour later with free entry visas and a hotel voucher. My American military status seemed to help things along for some reason. My well-spoken Nepali companion then protested and declared his treatment unfair.

"There will be no accommodations made for the flight from London," the staff member quipped. "His are the last visas we are giving out tonight."

He handed me our passports. It was 3 a.m., and we were told that we couldn't leave the airport until the customs officers returned from their half-hour break. We waited patiently and found it amusing when a man let two people cut in front of us in the customs line because "they are my cousins." Where was the German line-minder when you needed her?

The hotel bus wouldn't show up for another hour, and the turbaned customs official warned me not to let anyone know I was American – a bit of advice I appreciated. "Put your ID card away and do not talk to anyone," he said seriously. "Once people know you are an American, they will want to talk nonsense with you and it is not good."

"Shokran," I replied with a nod, which he returned. We would have to return to the airport at 7 a.m. The hotel bus didn't pick us up until 4:30 a.m. - perfect Arabian timing.

We arrived at the hotel and tried to dial Krishna in Kathmandu to let him know our arrival would be delayed by several hours. When I tried to direct-dial, I was told that I needed a $10 phone card. A shy and apologetic Sri Lankan worker brought the card to my door and showed me how to use it. I was able to reach Krishna, and was relieved that he wouldn't be waiting for us at the airport needlessly. No longer needing the card, I gave it to the worker and told him he could have it. Minutes later, he returned with several U.S. dollars to pay me the remaining balance.

"No thank you, you may have it," I said. "Keep it, it's OK." He seemed surprised, but smiled widely when he realized what I meant and then bowed several times. I hoped he could call his family.

Bleary-eyed and groggy, I felt like I was up for days when we finally settled into bed just minutes before 5 a.m. We would have to be up in a little more than an hour to take a shower and catch breakfast before taking the bus back to the airport. I shut my eyelids, determined to get some rest before the next long leg of our trip. As my breathing slowed and my sleepy eyelids rested firmly shut, a loudspeaker crackled to life outside.

"Allah u Akbar, Allah u Akbar!"[3] shrieked from a nearby minaret, ending my rest. It was the dawn *Azan*, the Muslim call to prayer – the first of five throughout the day. The often atrocious singing goes on to proclaim several more verses and can take several minutes to finish. More often than not, several mosques drone on at the same time. It's a sound that I've heard echoing in the early morning fog of Baghdad, Iraq, the hazy streets of Hurghada, Egypt, and the bustling town of Kemer, Turkey. On any other occasion, it would have been a moment of reflection and a bit exotic, but on this morning, it was invariably irritating.

---

[3] Allah is great, Allah is great.

The electrically amplified wailing subsided after a few minutes, allowing me to reattempt sleep. What I didn't know was that morning prayers are often followed by complimentary snacks for the hotel guests. As my eyelids sealed shut again, a loud knocking echoed outside in the hallway. "Refreshments!" someone called persistently, until told to go away. No one was interested in the hamburgers – apparently also known as "refreshments" in Qatar. I was interested in the refreshment called *sleep!* Frustrated and growing irritated, my head felt electric and dull at the same time, stuck in a bipolar limbo between extreme sleepiness and mental awareness. I cursed Qatar, looking over to see that it was already 5:45 a.m. Then, loud banging echoed from a nearby high-rise construction site crawling with skinny immigrant workers scaling the floors with absolutely no protection. Miraculously, I slipped out of consciousness for about 20 minutes, and enjoyed it immensely before waking up to a buffet of bread rolls and rubbery scrambled eggs.

At 7 a.m., there was no sign of the minibus drivers that would take us to the airport. The desert sun was already thickening the air. Half an hour late, our Sri Lankan driver whisked us away to the airport. Young female customs officials in traditional Muslim dress checked our passports without making eye contact. We checked the brand-new flat screen TV departure displays, and did not see our flight number listed. After asking a customer service representative, we were told that we would not need new boarding passes reissued, and that we would be departing from a gate on the second floor. My eyelids felt heavy and my head fuzzy as we walked around the bustling airport pumped full of chilly, air-conditioned desert air. We found a flight departing for Kathmandu, but were told that we were not on that flight, and that another aircraft was scheduled to fly out an hour later. Its departure gate would be on the first floor. We wandered from gate to gate until we found a gaggle of Nepali laborers in tattered clothes and western tourists sporting the latest in trekking fashion, standing in a remarkably long line that we happened to be standing at the end of. Our prospects of getting out of Doha looked grim.

We noticed that many of the westerners were forming a second line at the front, perhaps to improve their chances of catching a flight and desperate to avoid further delays. It seemed like it was every man for himself, as no one really trusted the airline or airport operations. I went to the apparent westerner line, and was told that I would need a new boarding pass, to which I resigned myself to the fact that such trivial disorder was normal in the Middle East.

Nora and I cleared check-in and were bused out to the awaiting aircraft after 30 minutes of waiting and coping with Germans elbowing passengers in the ribs trying frantically to get past others to board the terminal bus. They seemed, both at home and abroad, socially retarded when it came to civilized queuing etiquette. Small things like politeness and courtesy were totally disregarded. It's something totally contrary to the infamous German penchant for *Ordnung*, or order. I couldn't fully appreciate it at the time, but this was all part of escaping the gravitational field of the rat race we were leaving behind for Nepal. As soon as we plunged into our seats, Nora and I passed out in deep sleep.

2

flight to kathmandu

The flight to Kathmandu from Doha was absolutely packed, and we didn't enjoy the same frills that had dazzled us on the flight from Frankfurt. It was full of backpackers and Nepali laborers going home from their meager exploits abroad. Some of them wore tidy uniforms and hats that advertised some staffing company like those used to fill the service industry in Gulf states and American bases in warzones. Others were dressed in rags and broken plastic sandals. I distinctly remember one gangly fellow with a very dark complexion and large eyes that flashed with intensity. He kept a dirty grey cloth about his head and face as if to hide himself, and carried only a sack of belongings. He looked out of place among the five-star airline interior and wealthy tourists. For me, this would be a journey to a new place. For the laborers, this flight would mean the end of a long work cycle, rejoining their families with whatever money was left.

The cabin chat was interesting, with many of the passengers seeming to be seasoned trekkers. Two German men next to us described their exploits on Mount Kilimanjaro and their planned excursion to Everest Base Camp. Nora and I listened humbly, running out of subject matter to discuss, and dozed off somewhere over Pakistan. I tried to imagine how Kathmandu would look, how it would smell, and how the people would act. But aside from fuzzy and clichéd descriptions from the travel guides I had thumbed through, I really didn't know what to expect.

After six hours of flying, our five-star bus in the sky descended into the Kathmandu Valley. Rumor had it that those sitting on the left side of the plane could see the Himalayan range and Mount Everest. Necks craned and mouths opened as Nepalese and westerners alike drew close to the windows for a peek. Nora and I were sitting in the middle aisle and caught only slight glimpses of passing peaks in a hazy sky. Maybe it was my lack of sleep, but it all seemed like a dream, but the main landing gear striking the runway was enough to remind me it was real, and that two weeks of exploration were about to begin. As we taxied towards the terminal, I could see the rich browns and greens of the fields near the airport. I saw little concrete houses stacked like matchboxes in random places, with blankets hanging from their windows. It looked more like how I imagined India to be than a Himalayan kingdom in the sky. It was subtropical and earthy; the air on the tarmac was warm, and the Himalayan range was hidden by a thick seasonal haze.

Kathmandu's Tribhuvan International Airport possesses the physique of an international airport but is frozen in the 1980s with its brown interior accents and brick walls. Even so, the airport is an achievement when considering how difficult it must have been to build the facility with Nepal's limited supplies and logistical challenges. As Nora and I walked towards customs and stood in line with a large group of tourists waiting to apply for their tourist visas, the electricity in the building suddenly shut off and with it the immigration computer screens and overhead lights. I quickly assumed that power outages were a fact of life, as they were in Baghdad. We waited patiently as customs officials worked with pen and paper to process everyone.

I found myself almost begging for German efficiency, bland as it is, as Nora and I paid our visa fee and went to another line to have our passports endorsed. Behind a wooden counter, two lazy officials sluggishly reviewed passport information, and took their time placing the visa stickers. After my passport was processed, one of the customs officials inexplicably left while the other official sat idle. The tourists in line looked at each other in disbelief and frustration. The line came to a stop and did not begin to move again until 20 minutes later when the man returned and went back to affixing visa stickers. I understood we were no longer in the West. Needless delays and inefficiency were simply unpleasant facts. That was even true in a rich country like Qatar. For Nora, it was a bit frustrating and baffling. I was reminded of my time in Iraq. There is nothing a westerner can do to change the lifestyle, so it's better to adjust to it and stop living life by the hour. That is exactly why I left my watch at home whenever I traveled East.

It wasn't much longer until we were reunited with Krishna, our host, who was waiting at the arrival hall. We claimed our rucksacks from a rudimentary rubber conveyor belt and were approached by several people asking to assist us right as I spotted Krishna through the crowd of faces. He raised his hands and smiled warmly as he weaved his way towards us through the tourists. It was fantastic seeing a familiar face in such a new land. We had last seen each other in Frankfurt, and in this moment, the dream of going to Nepal suddenly became reality. A promise made became a promise kept. We were in Nepal among friends. My jetlag was quickly dissipating and my head clearing. It was time to live the moment and engage this new culture to the fullest.

Krishna greeted Nora first, and then with true back-slapping American etiquette, I heartily greeted Krishna with genuine happiness, and gave him a big hug despite his initial offer of a handshake. I knew there must have been a local customary greeting, but I would have to learn that later. Krishna led us towards the exits, where throngs of people and taxi drivers waited to spring on any westerner for business, or to make a rupee or two carrying luggage. Waiting there among them was Jenash, Krishna's son. We had corresponded with him by e-mail in the weeks leading up to the trip and were glad to finally meet him. Despite the hectic crowd and an urgent sense that we should leave the area as soon as possible, Krishna and Jenash stopped for a moment to present us each with a necklace of fresh marigold flowers. It was a customary welcome gift and much appreciated, as the natural aroma perfumed my senses and signaled our true arrival in Nepal.

We walked into the parking lot with our rucksacks and were surrounded by an entourage of miscellaneous Nepalese taxi drivers, handlers, and God knows who else. I was reminded of landing in Hurghada, Egypt, in 2005, where throngs of unemployed men and boys desperately flung themselves upon western tourists, hoping to earn some small change for carting their luggage. Not only was this hysteria annoying as a westerner, but it was also annoying for Krishna, who snapped at them to leave us alone before negotiating with the driver of a tiny beat-up taxi. A fare agreement was reached, and we stuffed our rucksacks in the trunk before getting in. The interior hadn't been cleaned in years and colorful Hindu art, along with tasseled window trim, was plastered willy-nilly in the front. We rolled away through the crowded parking lot, and Jenash followed us on a motorcycle while we chatted to Krishna in the front seat. The driver drove from the right side of the car as stickers of Canadian mascara queen Avril Lavigne stared back at me from his dusty sun visor. I saw images of Avril all over Nepal, perhaps more than any other Western pop icon. Snoop Dogg came in a distant second place, and I was reminded of the ubiquitous Britney Spears and Shakira images in Baghdad.

The roads were teeming with eccentrically decorated Tata lorries spewing diesel exhaust, motorcycles weaving fearlessly through traffic, food carts pushed by young boys, and cows walking freely among the flurry of Kathmandu's evening rush. With my window rolled down, the evening air blew through my hair as we passed shop after shop and multistoried buildings plastered in advertising for local private academies, soft drinks, internet services, and more. Kathmandu was alive, it was colorful, and it was like nothing I had ever seen before. The density of people and vehicles surging into one tidal mass with an occasional dog or cow must be unique to this part of the world, I thought to myself. Slowly but surely, I was coming to know what I could previously only imagine – and I liked it.

Arriving at Krishna's house was a special experience as guests from the West. We walked through the modest garden of his multistory house as Pepsi, their dog, barked suspiciously at us, despite our friendly gestures towards him. Children and people sitting on the balconies of neighboring houses watched us curiously, giggling and smiling when we made eye contact. We were a curiosity, a minority, travelers from the land of Avril Lavigne and Marlboro. As we made our way up the steps of Krishna's home, the sun set on Kathmandu. His wife, Triza, and their young domestic helper, Shrawan, assisted us with our bags, and led us to the door. Upon entering, we dropped our bags and exchanged greetings with the entire family.

Triza was very pretty, despite her older age. She wore a colorful, flowing red *shalwar kameez*[1] and glass bangles around her wrists. She smiled widely as she led us to the guest room along with Krishna. Their home was quite ordinary and decorated with family photos, Hindu religious images, and random decorations Krishna had brought back from his travels abroad. In the guest room, several mattresses sat on the floor – the equivalent of couches in the West. Nora and I took our seats on the mattress, and I promptly crossed my legs Indian-style. Krishna returned the gesture with a laugh.

"Look at you!" he chuckled. "You are sitting like you have been here before!" I appreciated his attention and smiled back. It was great to finally sit and relax with friends. I felt like we were with family, with people I had known for many years. Triza entered the room with Nepalese tea, smiling all the time and speaking to us in broken but perfectly understandable English. She radiated a motherly kindness and care we appreciated very much after a grueling flight.

Nepalese tea is unlike any other tea I've had. It's made of black tea, cardamom, and fresh ginger boiled in milk and sweetened with sugar. The aromatic drink has an energizing effect with its combination of caffeine and bite of ginger to awaken the senses. During our two

---

[1] Traditional common dress consisting of a long blouse and loose-fitting pants.

weeks in Nepal, this special tea blend became more and more familiar as we drank it at most meals with Krishna and his family, and on our trek in the Himalayas.

The Kathmandu sky was dark by the time we acquainted ourselves with the family and talked about what we would like to do during our visit. Jenash was a little frustrated that he couldn't whisk us into the city immediately to explore Kathmandu's nightlife, but Krishna made it clear that we should relax until the next morning. In the meantime, Nora and I were shown our bedroom on the top floor of the house. From the terrace, we had a full view of the Kathmandu skyline. The accommodations were perfect.

Before retiring for the night, we would need to meet a friend of Jenash who was interested in going with us on our trek to make sure things went smoothly. Nora and I were pretty sure we could trek without a guide, but Krishna insisted that it would be better if we went with friends. Taking his advice, we took a taxi through the densely crowded streets to a massive luxury hotel replete with interior mahogany carvings and fountains. The contrast between the grimy street life and the refined tourist hotel was amazingly sharp. Jenash led us through the lobby of the lavish hotel, past some elderly British tourists, to the basement area. There, a young man was passing time waiting to place calls as the phone operator in a small cell of an office. His name was Paras, and he smiled easily as he shook our hands and we got comfortable in his office to discuss what we would like to do, and how he could help. Paras was easygoing, spoke fluent English quite naturally, and was our age. He immediately seemed like a peer, a good friend, and someone we could trust. Nora and I weren't interested in taking a guide with us, uncomfortable with the thought of being some stranger's boss for a few days. We just wanted to go with friends, or by ourselves.

Nora and I were interested in hiking the Annapurna region and seeing as much as possible with our limited schedule. Paras knew this in advance, had already looked over some maps and bought a *Lonely Planet* guide for research. We decided that Annapurna I base camp was out of the question because of avalanche and altitude dangers. After some negotiation, we decided it would be best to fly up to the remote village of Jomsom from the lakeside tourist town of Pokhara, then hike downhill. As we poured over the maps together, Paras made recommendations and was thoughtful enough to have written up a packing list. Even though he was a university student, he planned and presented the information as a professional guide would.

Trekking in Nepal can be expensive despite it being a developing country. Estimating the costs for a week of trekking, Paras delivered some bad news. It would probably cost at least $1,500 for all of us, including a friend of Paras who would also be going along. I didn't expected to pay that much, especially as a compulsively shoestring traveler. Paras promised us the fee would be at least $2,000 per person with a professional tour company, which I totally believed to be true. After all, with so many Brits earning sterling and Germans bringing in strong euros, the dollar earners were at a disadvantage. Unlike the days of the *Hippy Trail*, many of the travelers we encountered in Nepal were young, high-powered professionals and the privileged classes. We were just a young couple trying to get some traveling in before starting a family and investing for the future. Nora and I recoiled in disbelief at the price, and seriously considered going on our own. We didn't want typical tourist comforts, and were willing to sleep in barns and take cold showers. Paras sensed our irritation, perhaps miscalculating what we were intending to spend. I felt uncomfortable discussing money with friends, but Paras agreed that he would scout the best prices and work with his contacts to find better transportation rates for the trip.

In some ways, it's difficult to travel affordably in some developing countries because of wealthy tourists and their kids who go to them. It gives locals the impression that all white people have lots of money. This inflates products and services for westerners, making them even more expensive than those same products and services in the West. For the wealthy tourist, that is a mere trifle. For the backpacker, it creates an irritating form of discrimination. Paras understood this, if reluctantly, and we agreed to meet again the following day.

discovering kathmandu

One of the most sublime moments in my life was the first morning that Nora and I awoke in Kathmandu. With the occasional exception of being awakened by the neighborhood roving guard, blowing his whistle to alert would-be thieves and residents alike that he was on the beat, Nora and I slept deeply in our comfortable guest room overlooking the city. In the early morning, I gently awoke with a sense of enormous wellbeing. Still not convinced that I was really in Nepal, I walked out onto the terrace into the cool morning air. Pigeons flocked overhead above the Kathmandu skyline, while offering bells rung out from thousands of households.

Triza was already awake and preparing breakfast. From a small closet nearby, rays of multicolored lights shined out from a slightly opened door. I peaked inside to see what the Christmas-like blinking was all about. The dark room was littered with dried flowers, splotches of powdered pigments caked to the floor, and a religious figurine surrounded by blinking LED lights. This was the family religious shrine – a place of honor and worship in the house. In the morning and evening, Triza conducted a ritual there involving water and bell-ringing at the end of the adoration.

Slowly, the family gathered in the kitchen, and Nora and I

joined them for a breakfast of rice and milk porridge with toast and fruit juice. We all sat at the family table as they quizzed us about the taste of the porridge, which was great. The warm and aromatic rice porridge was creamy with a hint of coconut and sugar. With a cup of spiced tea, Nora and I were enjoying ourselves. I couldn't thank them enough, especially Triza, who smiled as she made sure we felt at home. This was only one of many meals she would make for us during our stay, from curried eggs to baked fish.

"How did you guys sleep?" Jenash asked.

"Man, it was great," I said. Before falling asleep, I noticed so many sounds in the street below. The markets were open well into the night, dogs barking, people spitting, and someone whistling. "What's that whistling sound outside at night?"

"That's the guard," Krishna said. "They watch the neighborhood at night. Each person in the neighborhood has to do watch at some time. If you don't want to do it yourself, you can pay someone to do it. They whistle to let thieves know they are there and also to let the neighborhood know they are on duty."

"What about the police?" I asked naively.

"You don't want to bother with the police." Not sure what he meant, I later read about security problems in a Nepali English language newspaper. According to an article, the police show up late and are sometimes accused of being complicit. It reminded me of Iraq, where people mentioned that they were sometimes better off not getting the police involved.

Many of the infrastructure and civil services that we take for granted in the West, like police and public works, are simply lacking in many developing countries. Government doesn't function at all in the worst cases. People are fending for themselves and working with their neighbors to stay safe. I thought back to Frankfurt. It's a beautiful city and the epitome of efficiency. The city runs like clockwork, but at the same time, people in the region have a reputation among some foreigners of being smug, rude, and anal. Back at our apartment, dozens of people live mere feet apart, yet dodge glances or shy away from speaking with others. When an elderly woman fell in the street and struck her head on a curbstone in front of my kitchen window, Nora and I watched as some people walked past or stood around her, not knowing what to do. I grabbed a blanket and ran out to protect her from the winter chill. Immediately, I was told by the onlookers not to touch her because I "did not know what I was doing." Of course, inaction is preferable to amateur assistance in Germany.

"I know what I am doing," I replied. "I'm a trained U.S. Army medic." They looked on as I treated her, and an ambulance arrived after I asked a lady watching from a balcony to call one. Although cities like Kathmandu and Baghdad have very little in the way of public services, they do seem to rely on each other much more for protection and assistance. A neighbor walks the streets at night to ward off thieves, an uncle owns a car to help you move some furniture, and a cousin can help you get discounted bus tickets to New Delhi. Society in the East seems so much more interwoven and tribal than our sanitized, western life of independence and anonymity. Why should someone in Frankfurt get to know their neighbors or help an injured, anonymous person? The efficiency of the state is a blessing in most ways, but in some ways, it has replaced solidarity and interdependence. Why help your neighbor if some agency will do it for you? Why get to know your neighbor if you'll never need them for anything? Of course, the flipside of this is that resources in the West are generally distributed without discrimination or corruption.

All this aside, there is no better way to see Nepal than with the people who grew up there and love their country. As morning grew brighter, the Acharya family ran around the house preparing for the day's road trip they'd planned for us. I was humbled to think that they would go out of their way to introduce us to some of their favorite spots. Here we were, two tourists, and yet they were doing everything to make us feel welcome while taking valuable time from their projects to attend to us. We felt as if we were with family, true relatives.

"Today we are going to take you guys outside of the valley and up to Nagarkot," Jenash told us. "From up there, you can see Everest and the Himalayan range." It was to be a family outing with Jenash, Triza, the young house servant, Krishna, Nora, and me. As everyone went around the house to gather their things, a taxi driver waited below in the small alleyway in a tiny Korean minivan. It was a beautiful day for a family road trip.

We settled into van like sardines in a can and scooted away, weaving between pedestrians and animals on the main road towards the airport. With scooters, motorcycles, pedestrians, cars, and sometimes cows all flowing like a chaotic river through Kathmandu, I found it amazing that they didn't collide with each other. There were no traffic lights, rarely traffic police, and no road markings – but somehow, thousands of people crisscrossed each other without incident. I had to laugh as I thought of Germany with its dense forests of traffic signs and painstakingly detailed road directional features. If the U.S. has such a thing as the military-industrial complex, Germany has an equivalent traffic-industrial complex.

We sputtered towards the city limits for the less populated hills, crossing the black Manahara River and the shanty houses along its banks, home to the poorest of the poor. Cows sipped tar-black water from its littered banks, and some women could be seen washing their hair amongst floating plastic bottles just downstream from others washing their dishes. Multistory buildings along the road housed an endless array of private schools. Wherever you looked, there was an advertisement for private schools, some having names invoking visions of high academia like "Oxford Academy."

"Look at that building," I joked with Jenash. "It's covered in advertisements and signs. You can't even see the front of it."

"Yes," he laughed while translating what I'd said for Triza. "They have so much to advertise, but are all selling the same things!"

A lively hustle and bustle of impeccably dressed school children, with their ivory white clothes and pressed pant and skirt uniforms, chatted with each other against the provincial backdrop. Pretty women in colorful shalwar kameez dresses sat sideways on mopeds, chauffeured by male drivers with lightning-fast reflexes. Old men pushed carts through the maze of people selling roasted nuts. Tata busses belched thick black diesel exhaust as they weaved through traffic and smartly dressed men stood by chatting on mobile phones. A man without legs sat on a piece of wood with four small grocery cart wheels attached to it, and pushed himself along the road with his hands against the asphalt. The scene was a circus to my western eyes, but despite the chaos, there seemed to be a harmony in all of it.

The blur of Kathmandu's humid streets soon gave way to countryside terraces that radiated rich green colors in the sunlight, their patterns in the hillsides like emerald honeycombs stretching as far as the eye could see. In the distance, smoke stacks belched thick black smoke from the brick kilns that dotted the countryside like miniature volcanoes. As we began our ascent, Triza passed out small nectarines and miniature sweet bananas. I ate the fruit like I was eating popcorn at a theater – totally glued to the spectacle before me. Villagers masterfully created wood premium furniture in their garages worthy of a place on high-end western showroom floors. Women swept the dirt floors of their homes, floors renewed with new mud from time to time. Buses careened past us with passengers overflowing from their bellies and roofs. I had never seen anything like it before.

I became acutely aware of the inherent dangers of visiting the developing world when I noticed that the road was only little more than a car's width, winding, and lacking any guardrails whatsoever. Our reincarnation-believing driver confidently swerved around blind curves, tooting his horn to warn any oncoming Tata buses that they risked colliding with us – a collision that would probably send us tumbling into the valley. There was no margin of error, and that didn't seem to bother anyone.

"Does this make you nervous at all?" Krishna asked with a mischievous smile. Having been to Germany and America, he knew how safe we like our transportation – guardrails, signs, lane markings, proper clearance, those types of things. Nora and I nodded politely, confessing that we had seen our lives flash in front of us several times by now. "No worries," he assured us, "In Nepal, we are used to driving like this. It is normal."

Yes, of course, this is normal, I reassured myself. *Relax and enjoy the ride. There is nothing you can do about it now.* Just as I said that, a Tata bus, just like the sort I kept imagining would eventually kill us, swerved around the curve with the momentum of a battleship headed straight for us. He gave us the courtesy of a honking his horn while he was in the curve, giving us time to panic. Somehow, miraculously, we scooted impossibly close to the ledge and cleared the bus.

Perhaps out of sympathy for us, Krishna asked the driver to stop so we could get some fresh air in the pine forest and stretch our legs. We posed for a photo next to the minivan, and Jenash pointed at a pagoda-like building on the scrubby hill.

"You see that building up there?" he squinted as he aimed his finger uphill. I spotted a pavilion-like building overlooking the valley.

"Yeah, what is it?" I asked, not thinking much of the appearance.

"A few years ago, a drunken army sergeant came to this village and shot a bunch of people dead."

"What did he do that for?"

"He was just drunk, man. No reason, just drunk. So they build this memorial in the village."

Just then, another Tata bus passed by and proudly honked out a tune. Sitting atop the boxy, dilapidated bus were a dozen Nepalese lounging on the luggage as if they were relaxing on a park bench – a park bench five meters above the ground running hairpin turns at 30 miles an hour. Standing out from the crowd was a young western couple lounging amongst the luggage, soaking in the sun with the locals.

"You see that?" Jenash asked with a wide grin. "The tourists are riding Nepali-style! They must be Americans. Only Americans are crazy enough to do that."

I was immediately enchanted with rooftop seating and began fantasizing about being one of those crazy Americans riding down suicidal mountain roads on top of a bus. Imagine such a thing in the

West – riding atop a city bus through Philadelphia! As I began to think of upcoming opportunities to ride atop a bus, Nora – as always – read my mind.

"Don't even think about it, Dannyboy," she cautioned with a smile. She always balances out my irresponsible impulse with her prudent caution, and it's a good thing she does. Not wanting to push my luck with a wife I am fortunate likes to travel to odd places as much as I do. After all, we spent part of our honeymoon in Sarajevo, Bosnia. I conceded that bus-top seating looked thrilling, but I would put it on hold. It wasn't worth her becoming a widow in a developing country. She breathed a sigh of relief as we jumped back into the minivan and pulled back onto the road from hell.

Despite my military experience, Nora has still traveled to more countries than I have. Drawn to other cultures, she was an exchange student near Boston when we first met. Wanting to experience typical American life, she signed up to live with an American family for a year. But what is a typical American family? For Nora, it was a Muslim Nigerian family that emigrated two decades earlier. Later she would go on a geographical expedition to Syria, live with a family in France, and fall in love with Indian food in the British midlands. For her, language, food, and geography are fascinating. They are bridges between people she wanted to help build. Here in Nepal, she was in her element.

We reached the summit of Nagarkot, where it was possible to see Mount Everest on a clear day. Climbing to the top of a rickety lookout tower draped in prayer flags, we had our first peek at some of the most famous mountains in the world. Through the haze was a formation of white clouds high above the horizon. At least, intuitively I thought they were clouds. A closer look revealed a snowcapped ridgeline, nearly the whole Himalayan range. How could rock formations possibly reach so high into the sky, so high that I mistook them for clouds? I've seen the Rockies and the Alps, but they were mere foothills compared to these majestic stone cathedrals before us, these mountains of the gods, a place between heaven and earth, one last step before space and infinity.

While we could only vaguely make out Everest through the haze, it was clear there was more to Nepal than just the famous mountain. The entire range was awe-inspiring, enough to draw mountaineers and trekkers from all corners of the world to dance across the rooftop of the world set among a mystical culture. It would only be a matter of days before Nora and I would also be up in those wild hills, and seeing them for the first time was both inspiring and humbling. We knew we were in for the trek of a lifetime, a trek that we could have only imagined up until this point. But in that moment, we knew this would be unlike anything we'd experienced before.

"So what do you think?" Krishna asked.

"I think we are in way over our heads hiking up there! They are higher than I imagined."

"Of course! This is the top of the world. Those peaks are at least 20,000 feet and more. You know, I think it's better that you and Nora go with a guide. I will feel better if you do."

After seeing those peaks, I felt much better about that, too. It would be stupid to trek out into that territory without at least some local company. Jenash couldn't make it. He'd just returned from medical school in China and had to work a demanding schedule. Just taking a few hours off to show us around was hard enough on the novice doctor. Paras and his friend would be the best option, even if it was more expensive than we'd expected. It didn't make sense trying to save a few dollars when the extra expense could actually save your life.

"I agree. We are definitely going with Paras. Don't worry."

"Yeah, because if you get lost up there, you may not be coming back. That isn't the way to see Nepal," Jenash laughed.

On our way back to Kathmandu, we stopped by a mountain lodge nestled among farming terraces, ordered lunch and walked around the grounds a bit, where I saw bricks with swastikas on them.

"What are the swastikas there for?"

"Haha! No, no. These are not what you think," Jenash advised. "This is a symbol for Hindus. It means *Shakti*, a spiritual energy. This has been around way longer than Hitler. It faces a different direction.

Totally different, man. Lots of tourists see this and wonder what the hell it is. It's not what you think."

We sat around eating curry when a young English man pulled up to the lodge with a mountain bike. No small feat, considering we drove uphill for over an hour straight. He looked completely exhausted.

"Hi," he panted.

"Hi! Where are you coming from?"

"Left from Kathmandu today and this hill has already kicked my ass. And this is day one of 14. The diarrhea doesn't help, either. Watch what you drink, mate."

I looked over at my bottled water and thought about the tea I'd been drinking since we arrived. I was trying to avoid uncooked foods like vegetables and fruits without a peel, but that wasn't always possible.

"I've been watching everything and I still got sick. But it's worth it. This place is beautiful, isn't it?"

"Absolutely. We just got here yesterday, and it's a completely different world. Seeing the Himalayas for the first time was amazing. I had no idea they were *that* high."

"So, this is your first time in Nepal?"

"First time really this far east in Asia."

"Whoa! You are in for a treat, mate. This country is my favorite. The people are fantastic, the culture is amazing, and the scenery is, well, you know, amazing like it is right here. This is my second time here. I've been all over Asia, and this is by far the most magical of all of the countries. On the way up here, I stopped by a village procession and was invited in for tea. I felt like I had stepped back in time hundreds of years. There's nothing like it."

"That's what we hear. We're headed out to the Annapurna in a day or two. Do you have any advice?"

"Take a guide. Some blokes try the hike on their own and get lost, or worse, get themselves killed. And Nepal is a great country, pretty safe, but like any other place, you need to watch yourself. I know

I'm not the best example and should take my own advice, but people traveling alone get robbed or killed every now and then. It would be better just to play it safe and hire a guide." He wished us well and jumped back on his mountain bike, pedaling at a tortoise pace uphill. Looking at the hills around us, I figured he would be riding uphill for his entire 14-day trip. I was not as fit as Himalayan Lance Armstrong, so hiking downhill on our own trip seemed more attractive than ever. I made a mental note to ask Paras if that was somehow possible.

We descended back into the rush of Kathmandu city and listened to music from Jenash's MP3 player – traditional tunes from Maroon 5. He was listening to the same music we were listening to back in Europe. Now *this* was globalization. Who could imagine this being true 50 years ago? Music, movies, video games, and clothes seemed to be the same, whether we were in Frankfurt or Florida, Kathmandu or South Carolina. Globalization seemed to create a culturally homogenous middle class worldwide. There was always the local core culture, but atop it was an almost universal pop culture spreading digitally around the globe.

The family dropped Jenash, Nora, and me off downtown to get some last minute shopping in. We needed sandals, passport photos, and rupees before the big trip. Our first trip downtown was dizzying. People packed the old shopping district with its timbered facades and perfumed air. Goods spilled out into the street from packed stores along the way.

"Kathmandu is a city full of people doing nothing," Jenash joked. "You see, there are so many stores, and everyone is selling the same thing!" He ran in to grab Nora some sandals so we could avoid paying the tourist price for them.

Nora needed a passport photo for her trekking permit, so we visited a rudimentary photo studio where an old man in a vintage suit ushered us in and sat Nora down in a small room. Looking through a classic Leica, he was about to take her photo when the lights suddenly went out. We stood in the pitch black and heard him shuffling before a flashlight turned on. It was a power outage. He fetched a handheld flash and asked me to shine the flashlight on Nora's face so he could get the aim right. He snapped and wound the film, telling us to return later in the evening after he had manually developed the film in a dark room. In the age of digital photography, his little operation could have doubled as a photography museum. Here was someone still using his bare hands to produce images.

We met up with Paras and headed to a shop to trade dollars for rupees with a shopkeeper acquaintance. Like some kind of drug deal, we slipped over to an alley and traded cash. Apparently, this was not exactly legal. If his shifty eyes and nervous laugh were any indication, the exchange needed to be done quickly. Usually a rushed currency exchange on the street isn't a good idea, but we had done our homework, and our friends could verify the rate and quality of the bills. Plus, any tricks would spoil the social connections that brought us to him. He would lose face. In any case, the currency black market provided better rates than the official ones, not because it was funneled into elicit crime, but because it sidestepped official currency controls. The more a government could control the flow of foreign currency, the more they could control a currency's influence and the rupee's market price. If banks were limited in how many dollars they could distribute, or rates were adjusted to discourage exchange, you could still tap into the black market to convert cash to send your daughter to school abroad. This was a simple case of supply and demand. We got a discount rate on exchange for dollars because they could charge a higher one on the demand side for greater availability.

Cash in hand, we walked around downtown and stumbled across a train of men carrying a deity through the alleyways like an emperor. It looked like the *Arc of the Covenant*, except that it was draped in banana offerings. It was then I noticed what I thought was a young man in his early 20s sleeping on a rubbish heap. Some schoolgirls stood around him with crossed arms, and some people craned their necks to get a look. I took a closer look and realized this wasn't some drunken college kid passed out in the street. This guy was dead.

"What the fuck? That guy's not sleeping. He's dead, isn't he?"

"Yeah, let's keep going," Jenash motioned forward. "It's messed up."

Nora was walking ahead of me and didn't seem to notice. "You didn't see a guy sleeping in the trash back there, did you?"

"No, why?"

"Ah, OK. Don't worry about it. I thought you may have seen him." Relieved she really didn't know what I was talking about, and for once wasn't paying attention, I walked on and tried to erase the image from my mind. It was troubling for obvious reasons. Jenash hailed two rickshaws, and we jumped in. The driver stood up, leveraging all of his weight on the pedal crank to gain some momentum. This wasn't the latest mountain bike with multiple gears. This was a straight-chain effort, and their calf muscles showed it. We pulled into Kathmandu's historic Durbar Square to meet our other companion for the trek, Niraj. Walking past the temples, Jenash told us about the legend of a king who wouldn't eat his evening meal until he looked out across the valley and saw that every chimney was smoking. If one wasn't, he would send his men to ensure there was enough food for them.

Kathmandu's Durbar Square is one of three durbar squares situated in the Kathmandu Valley. The valley itself is made up of three cities: Kathmandu (city of glory and happiness), Latitpur, also known as Patan (city of craftsmen), and Bhaktapur (city of devotees). The current name for the square complex is Hanuman Dhoka, a name derived from the monkey devotee of Lord Ram, Hanuman. It is located directly in front of the Kathmandu Kingdom royal palace. The palace was originally located in Dattatreya Square in Bhaktapur but was later moved. Within the square are Malla and Shah royal palaces. The square has been a site for palaces dating back as far as the 3rd century. The beautiful Newari architecture there is renowned for its brickwork and intricate carvings of religious symbols and figures. The various names of the palaces and temples located in the square, such as Gunapo and Gupo, have led researchers to believe that the oldest palaces were built by Gunakamadev, the 10th century founder of Kathmandu.

Under the rule of King Ratna Malla, Kathmandu City became independent. The palaces in the square thought to be built by Gunakamadev were later claimed as royal palaces by the Malla kings. When Prithvi Narayan Shah, the Gurkha king credited with unifying Nepal, invaded in the 1760s, he also chose the square's palaces as a residence. The most prominent temple is the towering goddess Taleju Bhawani temple. The four-headed warrior goddess with ten arms was a protective deity of the Malla dynasties and continues to be worshiped by Hindus and Buddhists.

Curiously, adjoining the temple is a complex housing the living manifestation of Taleju Bhawani, also known as *Durga*. The Kumari Ghar temple was built in 1757 and to this day houses a prepubescent girl called the *Kumari Devi*, or royal goddess. The Kumari is revered as a living deity and her feet are not permitted to touch the ground. Selected by elders at around age three to five, one girl is recruited from many in a Buddhist clan to serve as a goddess until she menstruates or sheds blood. The selection process is very complex, involving rituals to screen out fearful candidates. This tradition still exists to this day, and a young girl inhabits the Kumari Ghar just as one did hundreds of years ago.

Ceremonies are still held within the palaces, and devotees have the opportunity to attend and worship privately. To this day, the square remains a location of great importance in the Nepal culture. Less than forty years ago, in 1975, thousands of Nepali people visited the square to see the coronation of King Birendra Bir Bikram Shah. Twenty six years later in 2001, thousands more Nepalese travelled to see the subsequent coronation of his successor, King Gyanendra Bir Bikram, enjoying another extravagant ceremony before the monarchy was abolished in 2008 making Nepal a republic.

Over curried vegetables, pizza and chocolate crepes, we met Niraj at a restaurant along the famous square. A graduate student at Kathmandu University, his focus was on environmental conservation. Our trek was to be a good fit for his personal and professional reasons. Getting away for a little over a week would be tough for him and Paras, so this wouldn't be a vacation, officially. No, we would be looking for the elusive snow leopard in the Mustang District of Nepal, a high altitude arid region bordering Tibet. That was our story, and we were sticking to it. Little did we know the meeting that evening would lead both Paras and Niraj not only to the Mustang for the first time in their lives, but to helping found an NGO, Tourism Development Endeavors, also known as TUDE.

Paras pulled out a map and a plan. Readjusting for budget and time, he suggested we head to the lakeside resort town of Pokhara and then fly up to Jomsom, the capital of Mustang. Tracing his fingers along the route, he said we could hike uphill to the holy temple of Muktinath near one of the highest trekking passes in the world. There, we could spend the night and then make our way back down to Jomsom, continuing on along the Kali Gandaki River past famous hot springs. At the end of the trail, we could catch a truck back to Pokhara and bus back to Kathmandu. This would offer us some diverse terrain, historic sites, and a downhill grade. We needed about 10 days to do it right, and it would be on budget. As an army guy, I was impressed with Paras' thorough plan. I was already convinced we couldn't do the trip without him, and at this point, we wouldn't want to – not because we would be vulnerable, but because we wanted to get to know him and Niraj better as friends. We toasted and folded the map away. Soon, we would be on our way to the Annapurna Circuit.

4

kathmandu sunrise

I thought I was delirious our second morning in Kathmandu. The gentle glow of the sunrise that woke me only moments before was fading again. I completely believed that I was dreaming and would awake later in Germany to go to work. *What a fantastic dream this is*, I thought…*waking in Kathmandu completely relaxed.*

I shut my eyes again, then opened them, realizing that I wasn't dreaming at all. This was real, and outside my window a saffron haze was enveloping Kathmandu Valley as a full solar eclipse began. I slipped from bed, put on some clothes, and went out to the terrace to try to take a photo of the event. It was an incredible feeling to be in such an exotic place and experiencing almost two sunrises within two hours. I shuffled into the main house and went downstairs to find Krishna wide awake watching the eclipse on television.

"Good morning," he smiled as he sat atop a cushion on the floor. "You see this?" he motioned toward the television.

"Yeah, I tried to take a photograph of it from the roof," I said.

"How did you sleep?" he asked.

"I slept great," I gratefully shared with him. "I slept so good, I thought all of this was just a dream and I was still stuck in Germany! I was about ready to go to work."

"Ah, no, no no, you're in Nepal! It's time to relax," he said, as the television switched from coverage of the eclipse to the Cricket World Cup in the West Indies, which seemed to have the entire country glued to their televisions and radios during our stay. "Today Jenash is going to take you into the city to see the Monkey Temple and some other sites." The Swayambhunath Stupa's nickname comes from the many monkeys – some of which are holy – that have made a heavenly home in one of Buddhism's most revered holy sites. "He and I will take you downtown first...on motorbikes."

Motorbikes were undoubtedly *the* preferred mode of travel in Kathmandu, which I came to relish as Krishna and Jenash whisked us along the city streets into the valley through the cool early morning air. For Nora and me, it was the first motorcycle ride of our lives. Traffic had not yet coagulated the city's main arteries as we curved through roundabouts. We passed gas stations guarded by men in military-looking uniforms watching large crowds of people waiting for gasoline. The crowds were only growing larger as their blank stares gazed off into the distance with little else to do than spend their time waiting for hours for a gallon or two of gas. Others walked their empty motorcycles or pushed their noiseless cars to the line. There was a fuel shortage, and like almost everything else, it had to be shipped in through India. Truck driver strikes, weather, and outstanding debts to the Indian Oil Corporation all made the subsidized gas scarce during our stay.

We pulled in front of an old white multistory building before Krishna rode away. As we walked through a corridor, some clay roofing tiles and masonry clacked through the air before crashing onto the sidewalk in front of us. I glanced up in time to see a worker wave back to me with a hammer in his other hand. They were renovating the roof and interior of the old stained building. A bit more cautiously than before, we continued into a large garden courtyard surrounded by single story, brick apartments. It was unusually quiet, except for the distant echo of a Hindi song with a high-pitched woman's voice sounding through a kitchen window overlooking the area.

We shuffled into Paras' cozy single room apartment, and Nora and I admired his remarkable sketches of The Doors front man Jim Morrison, while CNN International delivered the latest bad news on television, which I decidedly avoided listening to. I vowed early on that I would be news-fasting on this trip. After gathering our things, we went outside and up to the roof to take some photographs of the brick high-rise apartments, with their impossibly skinny frames. They were like Jenga towers wobbling into the sky. Nora used the opportunity to conspicuously bask in the sun, which was growing more intense with the day.

There is a funny thing about the Germans that I have never fully understood, as someone who grew up in the relatively sunny South. Whether they are lying like rock lizards on the shores of Ibiza or shuffling in from a cold German city street into tanning salon lobbies decorated with fake banana trees, wicker furniture, and plush monkey dolls, Germans love their ultraviolet light – and I can't blame them really. The winters can be harsh, not only because they are cold, but a low, gray overcast seems to hover over the country for months at a time. The bare, scruffy trees and fields seem to resemble a post-nuclear disaster landscape. Elderly Germans waddle with weary, pale faces to fetch bread against the backdrop. It can get depressing, enough to influence thousands of Germans to flee to sunnier spots like Turkey, Thailand, and Egypt as soon as they get a week or more off. Just when you think you can't take the black and white film movie any longer, Germany begins its metamorphosis into the picture book, fairy-tale land that it certainly is for a few warm months. We left Germany in March for Nepal, the gray season finally coming to an end, and Nora needed her sun on that Nepali rooftop. After being in Iraq, I learned to appreciate shade more than sun, but I sympathized for Nora. Jenash started laughing.

"How can you stand in the sun like that? White people are always trying to get in the sun!" he laughed.

"I need to get a tan on this trip," Nora joked back.

"See, Nepali people don't want to get a tan," he said, "We stay away from the sun as much as possible, otherwise we'll get really dark. White people want to be dark, dark people want to be white. This is a crazy world."

Moments later, Honda Hero motorbikes thundered to life in what must have sounded like the Sturgis Motorcycle Rally. As Paras, Niraj, and Jenash revved their motors, Nora and I jumped on to get our Annapurna Conservation Area passes and visit the Monkey Temple. I sat on the back of Niraj's bike, and was immediately tugged backwards as we accelerated past a few children playing in the street into a busy alleyway and snugly merged into the flow of motorcycles and a parade of women carrying vegetables, and men carrying carpets, hanging baskets drooped over their shoulders. As I craned my neck to see Niraj's speedometer steadily pass 15 kilometers (10 miles) an hour, he swerved to the left with Evel Knievel-like skill, narrowly avoiding a head-on collision with a car. My heart raced as I realized that we weren't narrowly avoiding collisions at all. This was just the way people drove in Kathmandu, and I wasn't used to it. Cutting to the left, then to the right, accelerating quickly and then coming to a halt in the busy streets were all part of driving here. Not surprisingly, westerners were generally not allowed to drive themselves around in Nepal.

We zipped along the bumpy, blistered roads with the wind flowing through our hair. Women in colorful saris blurred along my peripheral vision. We leaned into turns past shrines and temples as if in a dream. It was something straight out of a movie or video game, and it would only get more exciting later on in the day.

We first went to the Annapurna Conservation Area pass office where we registered our passports and indicated that we were traveling independently, as opposed to a registered trekking company or guide. Paras and Niraj registered separately for their pass, so as not to arouse any suspicions from the staff. Freelance, unregistered guides were understandably not allowed to get in on the lucrative trekking market without a proper registration, but in this case, we were all going as friends. There was a chance, though, that the authorities wouldn't see it that way.

Passes secured, we careened through the streets to a small travel agency that was somehow connected to a relative of the motorcycle gang. Like in other parts of Asia, it seemed that someone could get you nearly anything from a relative. You need a motorcycle? My cousin can get it for you. You need to change American dollars? Let my uncle do that for you on the black market. You need to get an airline ticket from Pokhara to the remote airfield of Jomsom, deep in the Annapurna mountain range? My brother-in-law has that covered. That is, if the power is on.

That was exactly what we were looking for, tickets for Paras, Niraj, Nora, and me from Pokhara to Jomsom. We figured, with only two weeks to explore, it would be better to fly up into the Himalayas and then hike uphill to our goal of Muktinath before turning around and hiking downhill for several days. It would be quicker, easier, and less expensive in the long run. We found ourselves sitting in a small travel office with two friendly men our group seemed to know well. The office furniture was Spartan, and faded airline posters showing Nepali destinations hung crooked on the walls. Paras and Niraj discussed our itinerary with the gentleman behind a late model computer who insisted no flights would be available, but seemed determined to find us one anyways. He wasn't going to lose face. He was a travel agent, and if he couldn't find us something, especially as guests in his country, no one could. With an expression of determination and serious business, he assessed the data on his screen.

"So where are you from?" asked a skinny fellow with a good American accent.

"Well, I am from the States and Nora is from Germany," I replied in a more relaxed manner than I might have done in Doha or Cairo. There, I may have answered that I was from Canada or Ireland. I explained that I had family in Florida, Virginia, and Pennsylvania.

"Yes! I lived in the States – in Virginia," he said with a grin as he reminisced about what seemed like a good time in his life. "I worked in an Indian restaurant as a cook and doing odd jobs to save money. I really liked America, especially the women! But it wasn't home. I had to return home." He couldn't have been older than 40 years old. "It's funny, you know, I have an education, but there I could make more money as a Nepali cooking Indian food and washing dishes than I could here in Nepal trying to find work as a professional."

"Yes, it's the great challenge for our people," Niraj interjected. "The economic situation here isn't that good for young people. So, we have people with degrees moving to Australia or America to do less educated work, just because they can make more money being a maid and send it home."

"He's right," the man said, "but you know, for me, I love my country. Sure, America is nice, but Nepal is beautiful. We may not have a lot of money or be a powerful country, but we are rich when it comes to the land's beauty and our culture." As he said that, the room went dark, filled with the sounds of computer cooling fans decelerating and electronics dying.

Paras turned around to us with a grin. "Power outage." It seemed to be a regular occurrence in the city that they learned to adapt to. The travel agent wasn't deterred, simply throwing his hands up in mock frustration and picking up a phone after all the data he'd entered was lost.

"No worries," Paras said. "He found us a flight, but he is going to have to call in our information over the telephone." We waited for the confirmation, and were issued paper tickets after handing over a wad of money. The flights were relatively cheap, and even cheaper for Paras and Niraj. Like some other things, there was not just an unofficial difference in prices for a foreigner and local, but an official one as well when it came to airline tickets. Our next stop, which everyone seemed really excited about, would be the Monkey Temple.

Overlooking Kathmandu, the Swayambhunath stupa is simply from another world. A stupa is a structure representing the virtues of Buddha's speech, body, and mind. They can be found in many forms, but typically incorporate a dome with a spire of thirteen tiers leading to a lotus flower shape. They may entomb holy relics or remains, or nothing at all, and range in size from a small monument in a village to a massive complex like Swayambhunath. It's not only one of the largest, but also one of the most religiously significant complexes of the modern world. The Tibetan name for Swayambhunath means *Sublime Trees*, a name referring to the many diverse species of trees growing around the complex. The Buddhist scripture called *Swayambhu Purana* tells how the stupa stands atop an area where a lotus once spontaneously grew from a great lake that filled the valley. It's from this story that some believe a version of the word Swayambhu comes from, which means *self created*.

The informal name *Monkey Temple* comes from a belief that holy monkeys reside in the northern sections of the temple. They are believed to be direct descendants of the ones that Manjushree, a Buddhist meditational deity credited with draining Kathmandu Valley, grew as head lice. The complex is a Buddhist pilgrimage site, but also revered by Hindus. Throughout the complex, there are dozens of smaller temples and shrines, some of which are more than 1,000 years old. The Swayambhunath itself is widely recognized as one of the oldest religious sites in Nepal, but its exact origins are still debated to this day.

At the base of the site is a dome, which represents the entirety of the world. On each side of the main stupa is a pair of eyes. These eyes are said to represent Wisdom and Compassion, with an eye between emanating rays whenever Buddha preaches. Each of the four lesser stupas also has carvings of the Panch Buddhas, known as the five Buddhas: Vairochana, Akshobhya, Amitabha, Amoghsiddhi and Ratna Sambhava. The main stupa in Swayambhunath was later renovated in 2010, only the 15th time since it was built, and used more than 20 kilos (about 45 pounds) of gold to restore the spire.

Despite being foreign to me, there was a sense of anticipation and reverence as we sped to the holy site. Once there, instead of taking the customary 365 steps up to the site, we darted on our motorcycles to the parking lot at the southwest of the compound.

Walking up the hill towards the entrance, it was difficult not to notice the sheer number of monkeys casually congregating on the grounds with their human-like facial expressions. It was the first time we had encountered monkeys outside of a zoo. Self-confident and not at all jumpy, these monkeys demanded respect and didn't like being challenged.. An older gentleman, presumably a Chinese tourist, engaged in a staring contest with one of the creatures, which suddenly shrieked and bolted straight for him. Visibly shaken, but careful not to lose face in public, he laughed nervously as he hopped away from the little beast. With some standoff distance, he then unwisely made cartoonish faces at a group of them. They immediately reacted and shrieked wildly while posturing for a fatal attack on the Tarzan imposter.

"You shouldn't tease the monkeys," Niraj warned us as we continued to walk up the hill. I turned around in time to see the man running away from the furry gang, who were now prowling on the sidewalk like patrolling soldiers.

Just short of the temple entrance, we passed some apartments, one of which had a window open loudly playing Snoop Dog. It was totally out of place. I noticed that Snoop Dog and 2Pac were popular with many youths in the city. Their faces were sported proudly on T-shirts all over. I had to reflect for a moment, though. It seemed that for better or worse, American culture had become a world culture for the middle class, from music to dress. I wondered if Americans knew that some of our staple exports included Snoop Dog and gangster rap. I love my country, but I resented the fact that our most successful cultural ambassadors were exporting gin and juice, shiznizzles, and beeeatches. It was something I had come to observe in other countries as well. Maybe I was being sentimental, but after years of traveling, I had come to the realization that our garbage is also a highly marketed commodity elsewhere in the world. On some intellectual level, a case could probably be made that the struggles sung about represent some of those in other countries as well. The rags-to-riches, get rich or die tryin' stories connect with youths. Even if you didn't understand the lyrics, which was more likely the case, the rhythm and tone, along with the visuals, all communicate a kind of undeterred male confidence.

This was probably more powerful stuff than traditional music. *Word.*

All those thoughts aside, we moved onto the main stupa grounds along with many other Nepali families and their children, under a clear blue sky. Unlike the gray facades of holy places in Europe I was accustomed to, like St. Peter's Basilica, Salisbury Cathedral, and the Cologne Cathedral, Monkey Temple seemed like a technicolor fantasy city; a kind of El Dorado in the East.

The stupa itself resembles the top hemisphere of a white globe topped with an intricately adorned, rustic bronze spire, like the terrestrial antennae from a Jules Verne science fiction story for communicating with the supernatural. Supporting the spire is a stone pedestal with Buddha's dreamy but piercing eyes looking from four sides, rimmed in hues of blue and red. Radiating from the top of the spire are strands of colorful flags fluttering their prayers into the wind, to be carried across Kathmandu valley into heaven. The different flag colors represent elements. For example, white represents air, red is fire, green is water, blue is sky, and yellow is earth.

On this particular day, believers young and old gathered at the wondrous site. Some old women arrived at the top of the stairs while genuflecting prostrate and standing back up again, slowly moving their bodies forward much like an inchworm does. For anyone who doesn't believe in God, these faithful demonstrated that God existed in the mind and the heart, just like love. And just like love, undeniable physical and visual evidence of God couldn't be produced in the same way as scientific proof of life. But, these people and others like them worldwide were evidence that God exists in the consciousness, and what exists in the conscious mind, and is perceived, is real for many. Here, God was very real. Coming here conferred a tangible benefit. It soothed the soul. It offered the promise of a blessing: a grandson making it into a good school; a daughter being happily married and having a child.

The temple grounds were a joy for the senses. Gongs, chanting, and incense-filled air carried the mind off in an exotic daydream. I walked along a corridor running my fingers across a row of prayer wheels and said a prayer for my grandmother and Iraqi friends still struggling as the situation there seemed to only get worse. I prayed for Nora and thanked God that I was lucky enough to find her. Taking in a deep breath of cardamom-perfumed air, I looked up at the prayer flags fluttering against a brilliant blue sky and smiled in a brief *thank you* to the big guy upstairs. In this brief private moment, I looked down to see a Buddhist nun smile at me and clasp her hands in a knowing *namaste* – a traditional greeting of respect meant to suppress the ego. Meaning "I bow to you," the gesture is made by pressing hands together as if in prayer and pointing them up towards one's chin. This is usually done first by a younger person, or one of lower societal rank. It was a ritual Nora and I came to enjoy as an icebreaker.

We toured the less magnificent parts of the temple grounds before leaving. The perimeter was littered in plastic waste and newspapers, which some monkeys held up as if they were reading them. Monkey families with babies on their backs seemed to run the place. Old men stood guard outside of lesser temples protecting food offerings from scavenging paws. Meant as gifts to the gods and not pet food, this conflict of interest pitted knife-wielding grandpas against mischievous monkeys. From the look of things, the monkeys were winning. Providing some entertainment for tourists, we watched one group of monkeys distract a guard while another slipped into a temple only to run out seconds later with an arm full of holy fruit. This was the essential symbiotic relationship. The gods provided the blessings, the believers provided the offerings and the monkeys offered to consume them. The huge primate population seemed more a twist of supply and demand than a divine plan.

Other aspects of the temple grounds were less divine. I noticed street children sitting in the shadows of boulders with vacant looks and bobbling heads. A closer look revealed curled up tubes of what looked like glue. In between begging and peddling Chinese trinkets, the kids would walk off to huff glue and other chemical cocktails. I watched one kid, no older than 10 years old, share a tube of glue with another child who huffed it deeply. His body wobbled, his toothy mouth parted, and his eyes rolled before regaining his composure. He walked away to peddle more goods, weaving a zigzag path like a drunk driver taking a sobriety test. Their swagger, their vacant stares, and their dirty clothes were a heartbreaking sight.

"Why are they doing that?" I asked.

"They aren't getting high for fun," Jenash clarified. "They are getting high because they are hungry. You smell glue, you lose your hunger. It takes the pain away."

"Can't someone do something about it?"

"It's a big problem. The solution is not so easy. Come on, let's go. There is nothing you can do about this today. It's part of Nepal. This isn't Germany."

Sitting in a tree overhead, a group of monkeys feasted on oranges while looking down at the street kids huffing themselves into a numb oblivion. Seeing similar scenes as this in the developing world, I knew this was a fact of life in many parts of the world, not just Nepal.

Jumping on our motorbikes, we departed for what would become one of the most fateful lunches of my life. Getting there was half the adventure, weaving through traffic and racing down narrow alleyways in some kind of Bollywood chase scene before pulling into the dreamscape that is Patan. The Durbar Square in Patan is located on the south side of the Bagmati River, which separates Patan from Kathmandu. The square itself is located in the center of Latitpur city and is one of the three Durbar Squares in the Kathmandu Valley. Many of the temples, like the famous Krishna Temple, were rebuilt during the reign of the first Malla King, King Siddhi Narsingh Malla, in the 1600s after the original complex was destroyed by Muslim Emperor Sam Suddin Iliyas. With origins dating back over 1,000 years, the square is one of the oldest in Nepal and a UNESCO World Heritage Site.

There are three courtyards in Patan Square. The first and most significant is the Mul Chowk. It is the largest of the three courtyards. In the center of the Mul Chowk is the Bidya Temple, and scattered around the courtyard are various Taleju temples. To the south of the

Mul Chowk courtyard is the Sundari Chowk. The Sundari Chowk was royal bathhouse intricately designed with a Tusha Hiti, translated as a *sunken tank*. Farther to the north is the Keshav Narayan Chowk courtyard, next to which stands the Degutale temple. The most notable aspect of the three courtyards is that the temples and shrines within each display gorgeous carvings and powerful, awe-inspiring Newari architecture. To create these terraced structures, Newari architects used a combination of brickwork and woodwork, a pagoda style that has been adopted across Asia as far as Japan. These tiered, tower-like temples and shrines, some containing multiple eaves, can stand over one hundred meters in some examples. This style even inspired the Tapei 101 design, one of the tallest buildings in the world.

The crown jewel is the Krishna Temple, commissioned by King Siddhi Narsingh Malla after being inspired by dream following a military victory. At the entrance of the main square, it stands out from the typical temple designs found in Kathmandu. Unlike the timber and brick pagodas dominating the square, the Krishna Temple is carved completely out of stone. This technique is thought to come from further south and resembles temple designs from the Gupta Empire in India, while incorporating the open air, tiered structure similar to Moghul architecture. The intricate carvings, stone lattice work, and 21 golden pinnacles are arranged on the eight-sided tiered structure, featuring detailed scenes of the Mahabharat and Ramayan, famous Hindu battles in South Asia. Guarded by two lion carvings, the site is an active place of worship for Hindus, with the first floor holding black stone carvings of Lord Krishna and two companions, Rukmani and Radha. Because of its uniqueness, the temple draws hundreds of architectural students and artists each year.

We walked the surreal square past merchants hawking souvenirs, looking like they belonged behind secure glass in museums. We joked that it was apparently everything the British forgot to take with them to the British Museum before 1947. Everything about the square not only looked ancient, it felt ancient. It seemed to rise out of the landscape, its unique architecture looking like something put there by a supernatural being. And there was more than met the eye. I scanned the rafters of a temple to discover little figurines peaking from hidden spaces with mischievous looks, more like mercenary Smurfs than the gargoyles of Prague.

The souvenir hawkers were all about business, but took their culture seriously. Nora and I looked through some copper Sanskrit bracelets and wooden masks to take back to Germany and add to our inadvertently eccentric home. One mask stood out. Nora picked it up to see if it would meet her exacting German standards for quality and price.

"Ah yes, this is excellent choice," the salesman said. Unlike in other countries we'd been to, he seemed genuinely interested in our selection. "But please, this is not an elephant."

Nora and I looked at each other and chuckled.

"No, no. We know this is Ganesh," Nora assured him. Ganesh is the deity resembling a human with an elephant's likeness. He's associated with prosperity and is especially good to have on your side if you're a businessperson. Nora and I were in the thick of a Beatles-like Indian enlightenment phase, which meant we were eating Indian food almost daily, listening to Hindi music, and amassing probably the largest collection of Bollywood movies of any white household outside of Russia. I'm not even sure how that happened, but we were enchanted by the Indian subcontinent. We knew Ganesh well.

"Yes! This is good you know! Many tourists ask for the 'elephant' mask, and this is no elephant!" he said relieved. "This is very special. You will take good care of this. He will bring you blessings."

We gathered up some turquoise-studded jewelry and other treasures before heading to a local restaurant for our infamous lunch. Better than the most potent Weight Watchers frozen meal, it was a lunch that would cause me to lose fifteen pounds in the span of two weeks. We settled into a small room in an alleyway, and Jenash barked orders to a boy who dashed off. There was something exotic about being invited to a back alley "local" eatery. I knew I was taking some risks as a foreigner unaccustomed to bugs that the Nepalese had a resistance to, but those concerns faded away when the boy returned with a plastic pitcher full of white liquid.

"This is chaang, a traditional rice beer here in Nepal," Jenash said while filling our glasses a little too enthusiastically. "You are going to love this, man."

I've been to a bar or two, and this is how more than a few infamous stories began. I had a hunch this was the beginning of the real Kathmandu tour *a la Jenash*. I was right. Six glasses later, I felt high. The milky white water had a barley-like aftertaste, was slightly putrid, and reminded me of Newcastle Brown Ale. It was delicious, although at first sight, and seeing the residue-covered pitcher, it did trigger a bit of a gag reflex.

"Man, you are liking the chaang!" Paras egged me on.

"Yeah, a bit too much. I feel like I am levitating; like I am floating on air or something. Is there something in this?"

"Nah. This is just alcohol from rice, but it has a different effect than just beer."

"Yeah, the mountain people drink this to stay warm," Niraj added. "This is a real Nepali drink. You won't be able to get this back in Germany." And with that, our waiter dropped off another pitcher of the white stuff.

"Now we are going to try some real Nepali food!" Jenash exclaimed. Something in the way he said it made me wonder what mischief we were about to get into. I was too caught up in the novelty and chaang-enhanced camaraderie to really ask what "real" Nepali food was. By the looks of Niraj's and Paras' embarrassed and shaking heads, I could tell we were in for an Anthony Bourdain experience. If I was reading Jenash's mischievous smile and Niraj's and Paras' unease correctly, I would have guessed we were about to eat fried goat asshole or water buffalo testicles. But the trap was set, and before I could protest, delicacies were laid out on our table. The child waiter threw me an amused look that said "you sure you want to do that?"

Rule number one when eating abroad, or at home for that matter, is making sure your food is well prepared. In an incredible grand folly of traveler's instinct, and probably because I was high on chaang, I sampled a platter of water buffalo tartare. While Niraj and Paras waved off Jenash's invitation to the bloody, finely chopped raw flesh, I embraced it with bravado. I was going to experience Nepal to the fullest! Looking back at the celebratory photos, I wish my wiser self could go back in time and grab – no, slap – the spoon out of my hand. In hindsight, the photos look like sequences out of a *Rescue 911* TV show dramatization of actual events leading up to some tragic accident. Bite after bite, encouraged by Jenash, we feasted on raw buffalo flesh, and what Nora would later dub my "little friend" opened up the door to my digestive track and threw his bags on the bed of my stomach and unpacked his nastiness.

Water buffalo tartare isn't recommended in any travel guide that I have read, and probably for good reason. Like a smoking chimpanzee or dog that drinks beer, I thought I was simply being a good sport, just entertaining my company. Throwing caution to the wind, Jenash and I ate raw water buffalo skin in oil and chili pepper seeds. Holding a piece up for better inspection, the chunks of flesh looked more like a cross section of skin you might find in a dermatologist's office illustration. Below was bright, jelly red flesh, with an intermediate layer of yellowish fat, and a final level of leathery gray skin – with hair follicles. There wasn't simply a hair in my lunch – there was part of a water buffalo hide in it. I shrugged my shoulders and downed square after square.

"Man, I don't think that is a good idea," Paras warned benevolently.

"Yeah, it probably isn't a good idea!" Jenash agreed.

Uh? Why was he agreeing? He arranged the menu! "What are you talking about? I thought this is real Nepali food?" I said half-joking.

"Yeah, but he doesn't have to hike with you the next week," Niraj said. "We do!"

As always, Nora didn't let illusions of adventure cloud her culinary sense. She sampled only a tiny bit of chaang and refused to eat any meat, especially raw meat. To make things worse, she warned me with a wag of the finger that I was probably going to pay for my carelessness later – and she was right. Of course she was. Any wishful thinking I had about my bloody lunch was abruptly spoiled when Niraj and I excused ourselves to the men's room.

It had been a long time since I felt genuinely ashamed. When Niraj and I walked, or stumbled, outside and around the corner to piss, we entered what looked like a dark shed from the alleyway. As my eyes adjusted to the darkness, I noticed some movement by the concrete slab floor that was the urinal. I looked over to see small boys squatting, diligently washing dishes from a broken pipe that also served to wash away urine. They looked like the same dishes we were eating from at lunch.

Yup. My ass is getting sick, for sure, I thought. But more than that, I was extremely uncomfortable relieving myself with these boys washing dishes at my feet like trained urchins. It broke my heart. This was wrong. Niraj thought so too, I sensed. "Man, I don't like this with the kids being here. It's messed up."

"I know man, I don't like it either."

I suddenly felt incredibly guilty. We exited the urinal and walked back to our dining space. Here we are feasting on raw water buffalo, and there are kids literally working in the shadows in a room that doubles as the toilet. Shifting the conversation, the guys wanted to show me the main room of the restaurant where the meals were prepared. A young Nepali woman tended a stove range like a dance hall DJ surrounded by frying eggs, meats, and vegetable pancakes. The aroma was at once putrid and perfumed. The lady smiled demurely for the camera when one of the guys said that I was a photographer for a famous magazine that was featuring her cooking. That was true, except for the famous part.

As the sun set, we careened through the streets to Kathmandu Durbar Square for dinner with a group of friends of our hosts. The timbered restaurant looked more like an opium den once the sunset and amber light bathed the interior dining rooms. From the windows, we saw candles on the temple houses and smelled the strong scent of incense and curried vegetables. We all talked about the challenges Nepal faced.

"I don't get it," I said. "All of you are highly qualified and educated. You obviously love your country. What are the barriers keeping you from making a difference here?"

"Some of this is politics, and some is Nepalese people just not believing they can do anything about it. Only a small group of elites control the government," one young man visiting with us said.

"Sad thing, as you already heard, you can make more money cleaning houses in Australia or working in restaurants in America than being a professional in Nepal," Niraj added. "Some of the smart people are leaving because of this. But we need them here. I have been abroad, but I know my home is here. This is where I need to be; to help my country."

"But what about the NGOs here? How do they help?"

"This is a complicated question," one answered. "You know, the government loves western NGOs because they provide services the government can't. They don't have to spend money if the NGOs are providing the services. This is good and bad."

"How would that be bad, though? Aren't they helping?"

"Helping, yes. But also helping the government from its responsibilities. The government can divert funding to wasteful projects, or ignore building needed services in some areas. They never learn to do it themselves because the NGOs are doing it for them. And sometimes, it seems the NGOs are more in it for themselves."

"I saw some of that in Iraq. A group of westerners running around in SUVs with probably more overhead costs and salary than the actual value of their contributions to the country. I got the impression that relief work NGOs could, if not managed properly and without the right guiding principles, become industries themselves."

"Yes, this can happen. This becomes a situation when the government suggests programs to the NGOs for assistance and then promotes that assistance for political gain. The NGO can tell their donors they are helping develop the country."

"But isn't that just a fact of life? Isn't it better than no help at all? Some money has to be better than no money?"

"Of course. I don't think this is all bad. But we are not beggars. We are not a welfare country. Sometimes this aid seems more for the benefit of the giver than the taker. We have very rich NGOs that bring young people from graduate schools in the West to help us here in Nepal. They pay the flights, put them up in nice housing, and they come tell us how to make Nepal better. Some of this is very good. But, what about us? What about the students here in Nepal that know our country and are just as smart as these young people?"

He was right. I never realized it until that point, but here I was surrounded by inspired young men. They were intellectually engaged, even patriotic. Jenash was a novice medical doctor. Paras and Niraj were studying environmental conservation. They were travelled. They spoke fluent English and were as much, if not more, plugged into current events and politics as any college student I'd met in the West. How did young men like these gain access to resources and levers of power to make a positive difference in Nepal's development? How could they break down their own cultural barriers to gaining influence, which were much more problematic than western NGOs? Could outside NGOs funneling their superior resources and importing their own specialists actually be propping up ineffective politicians and undermining local youths? These were questions that continued to echo in my mind throughout the evening and as I went to sleep that night. As we got to know Paras and Niraj better, I was convinced it was people like them who could help Nepal, not just western grad students living on compounds and nursing hangovers. The answer had to be somewhere in between.

kathmandu to pokhara and jomsom

The next morning, we got up early to meet the bus that would take us to Pokhara. Unlike the iconic Tata buses packed tighter than a Tokyo subway car, we would cruise in a VIP bus. That simply meant we had air conditioning, two people to a seat and functioning headlights. Niraj and Paras showed up, and helped us stow our rucksacks up top. They laughed, wondering what we brought for the trip. They only carried a small school backpack each, and they weren't even full! Who was I fooling? I wasn't the professional traveler I thought I was. I was a male caricature of the English colonial lady riding atop an elephant in British India begging for ice water. Nora and I even shrouded our bags in a protective mesh of steel wire and ballistic-grade plastic to prevent anyone from stealing them. I was almost embarrassed to be seen with the contraption in public, but I had to use it. It seemed to say loudly, "Hello people of Nepal! I am a paranoid tourist who thinks that you are going to rob me, so I am using this cage to protect my underwear and camera from your prying hands!" By now, I knew I had more to worry about in London or Paris than from Nepalese people. The rucksack security system was embarrassing, and it weighed at least three pounds, too. I completely deserved the looks I got for having it.

Soon, we were on the road with a small group of European tourists sputtering along and out of the capital. The route took most of the day along a 200-kilometer (125- mile) narrow stretch of road. Almost all of it ran along a river, deep in a valley hidden from direct sunlight. Like the trip to Nagarkot, the road was one great arena for playing chicken with Tata buses and lorries. With each hair-raising pass, drivers tooted out a melody from a special horn. It added a little charm to the whole experience. Often, I looked over to see people crammed together like a human puzzle, cheeks pressed against glass, butts pressed involuntarily against faces, and arms twisted in contortionist poses trying to hold on to anything to keep them stable. Indeed, we were on the VIP bus.

One lorry caught my eye, and when it did, I knew I was in trouble. The growling beast carried a load of about a dozen water buffalo. But these water buffalo weren't headed to the rice fields to work. They were headed to the city butcher. Piled high, their hides shiny with blood, they rolled past in slow motion. No refrigeration. No tarp. No U.S. Department of Agriculture quality seal stamped on their rear. I was pretty sure of that. I was also pretty sure the water buffalo tartare I ate earlier came from a similar source. Like the raw fish swarmed by flies I saw at a Kathmandu fishmonger's stand, this meat was probably sitting out for a while. I'm not a doctor, but when meat sits out like that, and you aren't used to it, there's a chance you are going to get sick. In the instant of having that thought, I felt the very first birth pangs of something within my bowels. Something bubbling and churning deep in my intestines.

We pulled into Pokhara, Nepal's second largest city. With some time to spare, we dropped our bags off at our hotel and headed to Phewa Lake. There, old women sat with their longboats hawking rides out to the mystical Barahi Temple island. The lake is Nepal's second largest, famous for reflecting the great peaks of the Annapurna region: Fishtail Mountain (Machapuchare), Dhaulagiri, and Annapurna. Each reaches well over 20,000 feet (over 6,000 meters). With our guide, we paddled under an overcast sky that turned the lake into a silver disk. Under a light rain, we moored at the temple to see a wooden pagoda gilded with copper and brass, housing a deity. The temple is devoted to Barahi, in the form of a boar, a manifestation of the female god energy, Shakti. Shakti is the creative spirit that shields gods from evil. The deity's boar likeness can be seen holding a fish and water vessel. Aside from its beautiful vistas, the temple is a major religious site attracting Hindu devotees from Nepal and beyond.

While walking the incensed, sacred grounds, I noticed a photo of a young girl in elaborate dress in some kind of advertisement. Was this a child marriage site?

"No, not child marriage like you are thinking," Niraj replied. "This is a ceremonial marriage. For religious reasons."

"So no girls are being married off to older men during all of this?"

"No, no," he chuckled. "This is a Newar religious tradition called *Ihi*. A young girl is symbolically married to the wood apple. This is about age five through nine or so.

"Yes, and the apple represents Lord Vishnu, the great Hindu god. This kind of apple stays fresh, so it symbolizes fertility," Paras added, "The girl is symbolically married to the fruit, and through the fruit to Vishnu, so that she is married for all time. Even when she marries a man later, and that man dies, she will still be considered married to Vishnu. This way, she receives a fertility blessing and never becomes a widow."

"But how does that explain marrying the sun?" I asked, looking at an illustration of an older girl in an intricately decorated red sari with gold lace.

"This is all very complicated!" they both laughed. "There is a ceremony where a girl becoming a woman is kept hidden away. This takes 12 days. She cannot see the sun or any men. She takes this time to learn from the elder women and how to do chores. It is like a bonding time for them. When the 12 days are finished, she can see the sun, and so gets married to the sun," Niraj explained.

The Hindu religion was fascinating with its thousands of ceremonies and stories. It all seemed overwhelming, but beautiful, too. My knowledge was limited to some tourist observations of Krishna, Ganesh, Shiva, and others. Their images were ubiquitous, devotion to them was intense and pious, and the rituals were rich in tradition and function. Even among the young people, I witnessed a modesty and prudence influenced by religion and honor. What they lacked in money, the country made up for in religious piety and friendliness.

After plying Phewa Lake, we took off exploring the waterfront. Like the Myrtle Beach of Nepal, tourist dives, trinket shops, and sports gear stores lined the lakefront. North Face gear, pirated CDs, and genuine Nepali handcrafts were all available at fair prices. We were looking for something authentic to take back, and later decided on a brass prayer wheel studded with rhinestones. Inside the drum of the wheel was a thick roll of mantras in Sanskrit. Despite the tourist appeal, the streets still felt special, with cardamom incense everywhere filling the nostrils, and the nonstop chanting *Om Mani Padme Hum* coming from everywhere. It was commercial, but also calming.

Something was wrong, though. I was salivating, and it had a bothersome acidity about it. My stomach was churning violently. I had the feeling that I was getting sick – *quick*. It was the same feeling I'd had in Iraq, Egypt, and other places. I wouldn't have to worry as long as I didn't get *eggy* burps. The repulsive, sulfuric mouth farts could be smelled across the room, and that usually meant there was serious trouble brewing in the gut. We sat down at a restaurant and I tried to hide my discomfort. If this was anything like I got in Iraq, it wouldn't end well. Worst of all, we were supposed to fly out the next day to begin our trek. Surely this wasn't happening.

Hoping an old recipe I learned in Egypt would work, I ordered a strong lemon tea and squeezed some more fresh juice in it. Slowly sipping the tangy tonic down, I felt the bottom drop out of my stomach, and frantically asked where the toilet was. Running as fast as I could around the building, past some kids playing in the alley, I spotted the outhouse in a panic. It seemed a mile away, but it was only feet. I lurched forward like a sprinter for the finish line, almost diving towards the small hole in the floor of the shack. Just a few feet short of my goal, I erupted into projectile vomiting. I'll spare the reader the details, but there was no happy end to this episode. Indeed, there was trouble on both ends. I had great faith in my lemony concoction, taught to me by people who know a thing or two about bacterial infections. As I stood in that shed, in a cold sweat, Dante's *Inferno* in my bowels, I realized this was serious. This wasn't going away. This had the potential to ruin the entire trip.

I wasn't the only one with a problem. Nora was feeling queasy, too. I knew I had a problem if she was feeling ill. She had a stomach of iron in all of the developing countries we'd been to. Plus, it helped that she didn't eat raw meats and other risky morsels. Nursing our stomachs and worried that at any time we would have to dash off into an alley, food was the last thing on my mind. Why eat or drink anything if it was just going to come back up again? Late at night, we decided to try to eat something. Niraj and Paras brought us to a small mom and pop *dahl baht* hut. The classic Nepali meal of lentil soup and rice with some assorted curried vegetables was excellent, but we were being polite. Nora and I sat on the floor watching a mouse scurry across the floor, knowing that we wouldn't be able to keep dinner down. I nursed a Coca Cola in posttraumatic fashion. Sipping a tiny bit and waiting for the stomach to respond. Repeat. The moment any tremors occur, cease drinking. The guys were worried for us. With only a few hours until our early morning flight, we couldn't be exploding at both ends, especially on an airplane. They scoured the city for drinking salts and diarrhea medicine. The stuff we brought from the grocery store in the West was no match for the beast within.

That night was the toughest we'd experienced in all our travels. Dehydrated, exhausted, and cramped from unusual bodily functions, I felt like my body was hijacked by some evil spirit, and Nora was near tears. We were up all night, violently ill with diarrhea and vomiting that seemed to never end. We drank gallons of a putrid mixture of hydration salts and downed Imodium pills in what seemed a losing battle. MTV India beamed images into our hotel room of young Indian women in colorful saris singing happily to suitors while I held Nora's hair. At 5 a.m., we realized there was a good chance we weren't making our flight, unless we could find some heavy-duty adult diapers and trash bags. I tend to be a mind-over-matter person. If you concentrate hard enough, I believe that in many situations, you can control your bodily functions and overcome many physical challenges. That morning though, it was clear that no amount of meditation was going to put our sickness on hold for a flight.

Next door, Niraj and Paras crawled from bed to prepare for our early flight into the Mustang District near the border of China. We exchanged some polite morning greetings in the dark. I'm sure we kept them up all night with what must have sounded like an exorcism next door. We were miserable and embarrassed. For some reason, Nora and I agreed that we should try to make the flight. Paras and Niraj weren't so sure. We took a taxi through the pitch black streets and out to an airfield. The perimeter was locked, and we stood outside under the stars waiting for soldiers to unlock it.

"Man, you going to be ok?" Paras asked.

"I don't know. I really don't. You have to ask whatever has taken over my body. You've seen that movie *Alien*? That is how I feel right now."

Paras shook his head with a sympathetic laugh. "You going to make it on the plane? We can figure something out if we have to wait." Niraj agreed.

"Yeah, I hope so. I've pretty much dehydrated myself and thrown everything up, so there's nothing left to come out."

"You know, I think that may be the buffalo meat. That probably wasn't a good idea. I didn't even eat that."

"Yes, believe me, when I saw the dead water buffalo on the trucks, I figured I was in for a treat, but I didn't think the treat would be dysentery. This shit is bad. I've got the *eggy* burps and everything." I nibbled on a Snickers bar, hoping the sugar would help. Nora was stoic. She never felt sorry for herself. Without any liquids or solids, she seemed stable, too. A guard came over and opened the gate and we walked towards the terminal.

As the light of dawn began to stretch out across the airfield, tourists and pilgrims sat patiently in the dark. The power went off right as I was getting into an old spaghetti western playing on the ancient TV – something about a horse stalking and attacking people. Outside on the tarmac sat two small turboprop aircraft with pilots and aircrews opening their hatches and inspecting their fuselages. I made an emergency trip to the restroom while Nora sat still and focused on keeping her stomach under control. Niraj and Paras stood nearby, wearing concern for us on their faces.

Miraculously, things took a turn for the better after a night of hell. We walked across the tarmac and sucked in the menthol-like morning air before stepping aboard our small Gorkha Airlines Dornier 228. The interior looked like a long minivan. I puckered up and said a silent prayer: *Dear God, Sweet Jesus, Saint Jude – patron saint of desperate and lost causes, and any other spirit able to ward off parasitic infection, please, please allow me to make this flight without shitting myself or explosive vomit. Amen.* Right then, a nicely dressed stewardess handed me a vomit bag. My prayers were working.

There was no turning back when we leapt above the Pokhara cityscape and roared directly toward some of the most famous peaks in the world. The Annapurna I and Dhaulagiri towered over us as we followed the Kali Gandaki River Valley north. We flew deep into the valley, boxed in like a mouse in a maze as rocky walls rushed past the windows. We buzzed dense evergreen forests, waterfalls, and cable bridges. Everyone was glued to their windows in awe. I briefly forgot about my health problems while Nora sat next to me rigidly. Her lips gave a slight smile, but she was clearly concentrating on keeping her floodgates shut while ravine winds tossed us around.

The green blur rushing by our window suddenly turned into clay, like the surface of Mars. Ribbons of grey, brown, and tan swirled among ragged brush rapidly rising towards us. This was the Tibetan landscape I'd seen before only in books or travel shows. Without much descent or warning, we slammed onto a runway in the bottom of the canyon and lurched forward as thrust reversers and brakes brought us to a screeching halt.

We made it to Jomsom without incident. Soldiers escorted us onto the tarmac. It was one of the most beautiful sights I'd ever seen. It felt like we were at the top of the world; like we were in an alpine wonderland, surrounded in all directions by impossibly high peaks. The crisp atmosphere was silent, like a vacuum in outer space. The blue sky took on a darker hue of high altitude. Nora and I held out just long enough. Just as we arrived at the small terminal building, nature called with a loud gargling sound from my stomach.

Jomsom is part of the Mustang District of Nepal, a barren region situated in a rain shadow. The village hosts an army mountain warfare school and several rustic lodges, called tea houses, for passing trekkers, but not much more. Its stone and cinderblock structures with rickety timber staircases stand like outposts on an alien planet, void of sound and life. It's both austere and beautiful at once, unlike any place Nora and I ever visited. Not even Paras or Niraj had been here before.

"We've been talking, and we think it's a good idea to take some time here and relax. Make sure you are feeling good for the trip." Niraj offered. "We have time."

"Yeah, that sounds good. Nora and I didn't sleep at all last night." I had a feeling they hadn't slept either, being next door to us. "I tried to fight this, but I'm just weak right now." Nora nodded. She's the toughest gal I've ever met, but there was no reason to Rambo up and try to take off into the hills. We had to respect the unspoken rules of trekking: respect nature and yourself. "And drink lots of Tang," Paras would say.

Paras and Niraj were already lifesavers – friendly, smart, and patient. Yes, patient. They were there when I decided to chow down on raw water buffalo hide with Jenash, who was nowhere to be seen now. They waited patiently for our stomach drama to settle, and excused our sudden dashes into the restrooms. They searched Pokhara late at night for medicine while other guides were out partying. Simply, if it weren't for them, we would be in big trouble, or more accurately: bigger trouble. We would have been incredibly stupid not to bring a guide. *Thank God we had guides and friends on this trip,* I thought, nursing a headache in the bright morning sun.

The guys found a rustic guest lodge nestled along the canyon wall. In what would become a daily routine, they searched out the best places, negotiated a price, and then called us in to register. Our first Annapurna guesthouse was just right. Comfortable beds, western toilet and shower with warm water, in-house restaurant, and a nice porch in the sun. I walked the dusty grounds and found a dead puppy mummified among some cans while donkey trains jingled past. It felt like we were staying in the Wild West. Nora and I took some curried potatoes and Tibetan honey bread before resting for the night. We were exhausted. We felt bad for keeping Paras and Niraj in the outpost town for an entire day, but any regrets melted away as we slipped into a cozy, deep sleep until the next morning.

jomsom to jharkot

I woke up in the darkness of the cabin feeling strong enough for the day's trek higher into the Himalayas, or at least I hoped. Nora and I had already lost one full day recovering from exploding bowel syndrome, and unlike the other European trekkers getting in touch with their inner selves in Shangri-La, I didn't have the luxury of a six week vacation to pace myself. That was one of the reasons we couldn't complete the entire Annapurna Circuit in the first place, which is a 300 kilometer (190 mile) trek around the Annapurna mountain range. This would have to do, and there was no way I was going to let my stomach stop me.

As I climbed from bed like a three-toed sloth, trying not to awaken the beast in my intestines, a garbled hissing sound like a muffled cappuccino machine came from my stomach, immediately followed by an uncontrollable urge to climb atop the porcelain throne before it was too late. I came all the way from Germany, and some microscopic parasite was setting up shop in my large intestine, napkin tucked under his chin, knife in one pseudopodia and fork in the other! It seemed like the only way to deal with my little visitor and still salvage something of the trip was to learn to adapt, to be a good host.

"OK, parasite, I get it," I thought. "You are going to be in there for a while, so what do I need to do to salvage some of this trip?"

"I'm glad you asked!" he said. "Look, the way this works is that I'll be sending you to the outhouse twice a day for the next few weeks, once in the morning and once in the evening. Just keep yourself well-fed and hydrated, and we should be okay."

"And what about the eggy burps that fill up the room?"

"Keep eating solids and those should go away. Don't even try meds, though. You won't be able to keep them down anyway."

I'll spare the details of what went on while this conversation unfolded, but let's just say it involved an inhuman amount of fluids and a sweat-drenched forehead. If this was going to be the new normal, I needed a strategy. I needed to structure it as much as possible, to not let it sap my strength. They say attitude is everything, and mine was to treat this hideous affliction like a normal bodily function. I wouldn't get upset about it, or let it distract me from the natural beauty of our surroundings. I resolved to simply go…once in the morning and once in the evening, filling the time in between with hiking my ass off. When I did have to go, it would be fast, without any self-pity, and then back to whatever I was doing.

Nora fared much better. With a stomach like an iron kettle, she quickly recovered from her double trouble and was up and ready to go, lacing her boots, half scolding me for eating something ridiculous like raw water buffalo and chuckling at my ongoing negotiations with what she called my "little friend." Surely, I deserved it. Ever since contracting E. Coli in Iraq in 2003 and vomiting once every hour for two weeks thereafter, my stomach was never the same. While Nora knew that was true, I was still in denial with my culinary misadventures.

We left our rooms into the cool morning air to eat breakfast with Niraj and Paras in the main house. The timber boardwalk creaking beneath our boots was the only sound around. Looking up at the stars, it felt like we were out for a walk on the surface of the moon at 3 a.m. on a Sunday morning. Ducking into the main room, we joined Niraj and Paras, both wearing concerned looks on their candle-lit faces.

"How are you feeling? Are you going to be able to make it?" Paras asked.

"I'll be fine, I think." I half-lied. "It's only hitting me in the evening and morning, so I should be fine. I'm just going to force myself to drink and eat normally."

Just as I said the word "normally," the sound of a draining sink emanated from under my fleece shirt. "Pucker up, Mister!" my brain commanded immediately. And pucker up I did, but something on my face must have given it away as Paras grinned and knowingly shook his head.

Rucksacks at our sides, all of us sat around the breakfast table in a room decorated by faded tourism posters tacked to the rustic cabin walls. The glow of the lamps reflected images of skiers and trekkers in kitsch 1980s sports gear alongside the photos of the hostess' parents. This seemed to be a tradition in most of the homes and guesthouses we visited. Portraits of dignified couples, the parents and grandparents of the inhabitants, usually held a place of honor, peering at you through history, their watchful gaze still keeping an eye on their children. Many of the older pictures looked like something from the Smithsonian collection, like a Nepali version of Abraham Lincoln or Geronimo dressed smartly and sitting perfectly upright next to a demure, young Himalayan woman.

The hostess was deferential without showing any exaggerated displays of servitude, a condition we often noticed as western tourists in foreign countries. This always made me uncomfortable, especially being relatively young and completely undeserving of any special treatment simply based on where I came from. As an American, it's the content of character that I prefer to guide social interactions, rather than any entitlement or privilege. So I was relieved when *Didi*, the generic nickname and term of endearment for women, similar to calling them sister, took time to chat with us while placing hot coals under the table draped in a heavy cloth. She then set the table with fresh Tibetan fried bread and wild honey. I wondered if the founder of

Krispy Kreme had ever been to Nepal? Surely, this would have inspired his sweet invention!

Despite the cold morning, we were able to keep cozy while coals warmed our booted feet under the table covered by a heavy yak wool blanket. Out in the darkness of the main road sounded a dull tin can-like clanking, growing louder and louder. It was a donkey train making its way into the pitch-black town like a ghost ship ringing its bell in the doldrums on a starless night. It's essential to move the mules early in the morning to avoid high winds and temperatures, always oppressive and violent in the afternoons at this point in the Kali Gandaki Valley. That was exactly why we were looking to depart as soon as possible for the uphill trek.

None of us knew exactly what to expect on the way ahead. Neither Niraj nor Paras had ever been to this remote part of Nepal before. However, that didn't keep us from stepping into what looked like a film set for a Wild West boomtown, dusty main street surrounded by shops made of petrified-looking wood and windows chocked full of backpacker goods like Tang and medicine, and heading north. In the early morning light, we reached the outskirts of Jomsom, passing a formation of intense Nepali paratroopers running in formation. Emotionless guards looked at us, fingering their rifle triggers.

"I don't miss that one bit," I muttered under my breath, thinking back to morning exercises and gate guard duty in the Army years before.

The path was tame and level, nothing like it would become later. At this point, we were still relatively within civilization. We passed small children walking to school in immaculate uniforms, gathering in simple buildings emblazoned with signs of sponsoring charities and NGOs. Some waved hello, but the novelty of westerners walking through their neighborhood had faded long ago.

With the village behind us, we entered a wide-open valley littered with scree and a broad-threaded river that fed into the Ganges. Aside from a few lone porters carrying loads the size of bathtubs by

straps on their foreheads, we were completely on our own. Hiking in
what was essentially a riverbed about 10 or more football fields wide,
the trail was hard to discern. It was more just a general direction
between water to one side and cliffs to the other. Following what we
thought was a trail, we went up the side of the valley to find an
impassable section. Spread-eagle across a rock face with a fifty-foot
drop beneath me, Paras and I tried to force our way around a bend in a
rock wall that obstructed our way, but realized how stupid that was
with our packs on. About this time I realized that the need to advance
forward was a magnetic, sometimes irrational force. Nora and I would
encounter it again later in the trek when we navigated trails as if in a
trance, purely focused on maintaining momentum, and ignoring what
were clearly trails that punished any tiny error with severe injury or
death.

Walking in the valley was like entering the gates at the end of
the world, surrounded by the 17,224 foot (5,250 meter) Dhampus and
26, 246 foot (8,091 meter) Annapurna I. The rocky sides of the valley
reaching into the deep blue sky looked like marble cake with finger
print-like patterns. They showed how layers of rock had been kneaded
and twisted for thousands of years by the hands of time in a slow-
motion collision of the Indian subcontinent with Asia. Taking a water
break, we turned over some rocks to find what looked like alien life
forms in black stone. The fossilized nautilus shells were part of what
used to be a seabed pushed into the sky by tectonic forces. The ancient
seabed now formed a layer of sedimentary rock full of brittle seashells,
making up part of the marble cake layers high in the Himalayas. It was
the last place I would have expected to find seashells.

We learned that the black stones we found were actually
considered holy. The black nautilus fossils are also known as *Shaligram
Shila*, *Sila*, or just *Shila*. They are considered a form of Vishnu, the four-
armed Hindu god known as the Supreme Being. The holy stones are
famously found in the Kali Gandaki River and surrounding valley, itself
considered a holy place in Hindu scripture. The name *Shaligram Shila* is
translated as Vishnu Stone, as *Shila* is the common word for stone,

while Shaligram is a fairly uncommon name of the Hindu god Vishnu. Shaligram, in Hinduism, can also be called *Salagrama*, a name referring to the small village that sits along the banks of the river. They are sometimes called *murti*, which means it is a sacred object of devotion when designated for that purpose. Other murti may include images and statues in temples that are offered for devotional purposes. For example, the Ganesh carving that Nora and I bought in Kathmandu represents the Hindu god with the elephant-like image, but it is not murti because it was not presented for devotional purposes. If it were hosted in a temple and given proper honors, then it may become murti if it met the traditional conditions required.

In Hinduism, *Tulsi*, known as Holy Basil, is a plant very closely related to the worship of Shaligram Shila. Hindu legend states that at one point in time Saraswati, the Hindu goddess of the arts, music, science and knowledge, cursed Lakshmi, the beautiful goddess of wealth and prosperity, turning her in to a Tulsi plant and binding her to earth for all eternity. Vishnu intervened, telling Lakshmi that she would be bound on earth as a tulasi (another name for Holy Basil) until the waters of the Gandaki River flowed from her body. Vishnu said that he would wait by her side on the banks of the river, in the form of a stone, until this took place. The stone that Vishnu became was the Shaligram Shila. Ever since then, they have been sacred to devotees of the Hindu faith.

Shaligram Shila are easily identifiable with their two key visual qualities. The first is the unique coloring of the stone, which can be black, red or a mixture. The second is the marking on the stone, thought to be fossilized imprints of Vishnu's mace, lotus, conch and *chakra*, or disc. A biologist would notice that the black stones resemble a nautilus shell, and they would be correct. They are passed down to each generation, kept within the family that originally found the stone. The sacred relics are never sold or bartered with and cannot be bought. A devotee in possession of one of these precious stones must adhere to strict rules of faith. The stones are not to be placed on the ground, nor touched without the devotee first bathing thoroughly. The worshipper of the stone is also limited to eating only *Prasad*, foods that are gifted to Vishnu and then passed to his followers, and is forbidden from partaking in impure practices such as gluttony or deviance. Selling or dishonoring the stones, especially as murti, is a mortal sin, punishable by banishment in hell.

Just as we were sifting through these ghosts of the past, a twin-engine turboprop passenger plane buzzed overhead into the canyon and pulled a tight banking maneuver. The morning flight from Pokhara was clearly in a hurry to get on the ground before the winds picked up, and was opting to approach the airfield from the north instead of straight in from the south, as we had. Pulling more than a full 180-degree hairpin turn, the plane looked like a toy, barely missing the opposite side of the canyon by a football field or so before dropping its landing gear and flaps, as if in a combat landing configuration. In May 2012, 15 people were killed when their airplane struck the mountainside in a similar approach. Like everything else here, there was no margin for error.

Our rucksacks reflected that concern. Our bulging 40-liter bags were packed to the brim with gear to meet every imaginable climate, minor medical emergency, and recreational activity. This was in contrast to Paras and Niraj with their half-empty schoolboy backpacks and sneakers. They must have thought we were either professionals or slightly eccentric at first, but as we ascended steadily for a few hours, they asked if they could carry our bags. Now, I have always prided myself on carrying my own bag, if not an additional one for someone in need, but by now the sun was beating on us and our guides insisted. At this time, I realized that our hiking poles, purchased especially for this occasion, were accomplishing very little and looking a little ridiculous. Panting and sweating out what fluids I had left in my body, I reluctantly lowered my 40-pound rucksack into Paras' hands, and suddenly felt like I was levitating.

The truth was, despite being in the Army and hiking in the Alps and other places, I was still a packing novice. Like a balloonist casting away sandbags to gain altitude, I was seriously considering donating half of my well-intentioned stuff to the next settlement. I still hadn't learned to pack light, only the essentials, to gain heat from layers, and to do laundry on the way. I remember being a young private hiking around the backwoods of the Taunus in Germany with three days of water strapped to me, and a 20 CD wallet among other things, not realizing at the time it would be better just to buy provisions along the way and listen to the radio instead. When Paras took my bag, I swore I would never be so foolish again.

After an hour of walking up the side of the valley, we reached a lookout point, like none I had seen before. To the north was a great pass leading to the Upper Mustang region, a mysterious and even more rustic area bordering on China with monastic caves and very few tourists. You needed special permission to go there, and a professional guide. To the west was a zigzagging trail that looked like a form of South American land art. Running from the bottom of the valley all the way to the top, it was one of the only ways to Dolpo, a place that Niraj and Paras insisted would be both very difficult to reach, and exotic. From our vantage point, the monotonous adobe tone landscape, bone dry and seemingly soundproof, transformed into a patchwork of colors. In the valley were the vibrant green patches of Kagbeni's meager fields, brilliant snow-capped peaks along the horizon, and turquoise blue skies. We were transitioning from the dirty valleys to the heavens.

Continuing our ascent, this time without hiking sticks, we reached a small outpost run by an old Nepali woman. She hurried around the place barking orders viciously at some of her help, pausing to smile at us while tending to a pot simmering on a solar oven. At these altitudes, wood is in short supply, partly because of nature and partly from overconsumption through the years. A European we met in the garden sipping on Coca Cola was, according to him, one of the inventors of the oven, something that looked like a satellite dish made of stainless steel. It concentrates the rays of the sun on a pot holder, and can boil water in just a few minutes, all without electricity. The gentleman seemed well known to the locals, and told us that he raises money for the ovens, bringing them to remote places in Nepal each year.

We reached the snowline by midafternoon, continuing to climb higher into the ridgeline under a dome of brilliant blue sky. The snow looked like bubble bath foam scattered across a gravel parking lot, spotted with twiggy bushes void of any life. Pitiful-looking mountain goats roamed the area, plucking away at the lifeless shrubbery with sunken heads and bloated bellies. Looking out across the canyon, I noticed deep grooves on the opposite side looking like folds of clay-colored elephant skin reaching hundreds of feet into the air, an effect caused by a millennium of erosion. Looking a bit harder, though, there were dozens of caves carved into the rock faces. Surely, many of them were unexplored. It seemed they were also inhabited, by the raptor calls echoing eerily from below.

A Himalayan Condor looks like a small airplane from afar. As one neared us, its wings fully outstretched in full sail across the mountain breeze and masterfully adjusting the pitch of the wings, I jokingly wondered if I was in such poor form that my silhouette was attracting scavenging predators. Maybe I was, because the creature took up a holding pattern directly overhead as we made our way along the dusty trail. The grade remained constant as we climbed, but my heart rate increased noticeably, my mouth became drier, and a faint headache began to throb in my skull.

"The condor is a very special creature in the mountains, especially for the people," Niraj explained as we took a photo break. "The locals bring their dead up to the hills to be eaten by the vultures. They believe they carry the spirit into the sky."

This practice differed distinctly from the riverside funeral pyres practiced in lower elevations. With little wood available at this altitude, around 10,000 feet (3,000 meters), it couldn't be wasted on cremating the dead when harsh winters required that food and heating needed to be taken care of. Especially extraordinary about this feathered funeral was that a family member first dismembered the deceased into quarters with a knife. The birds, knowing the drill, would then be allowed to swoop down and consume the remains. While this seemed revolting as it was explained to me, slicing a corpse open and pumping it full of chemicals, putting it into an expensive box and burying it in the ground probably sounds strange to Nepalese living in the mountains. Why would anyone waste that much money?

Business was good on the trail, if the motley crew of porters and handymen making their way up and down the trail was any indication. One fellow we kept running into was carrying electrical supplies and dozens of egg cartons packed into what looked like a large, rusty rabbit cage hanging by a strap around his forehead. Many of these men looked like they were of retirement age, their skin aged like leather and tanned deep red. The contrast between the whites of their eyes and dark faces, made even darker by the rush of blood to their heads, looked like inset ivory. Although they carried loads a Navy Seal would consider out-of-the-question in terrain like this, they flashed gentle smiles passing by. Looking closely, you could see the shuddering of their necks, their poorly-shoed feet searching for firm footing among the rocks, but most importantly, a focus that alternated between a Vietnam vet's *thousand yard stare* and an *eye on the prize* gaze of determination. These mountain men were hard, much harder than any Hollywood caricature of strength, be they gun-toting muscle men or emo-gunslingers in trench coats – what bullshit. Here was human strength incarnate at work, not simply on display. These men were pushing insane limits, carrying loads of at least 80 pounds (about 40 kilos), often more, uphill for miles, sometimes in no more than shower shoes they scored from a tourist. From six cases of Coca Cola in glass bottles to two-dozen live chickens, we watched each passing Himalayan Hercules carry impossible loads over terrain that would have had most people turning around and going home.

Continuing our march, I wondered where home would be for the night. It was nearing midafternoon and my muscles ached, although my bowels were cooperating quite well. It seemed the truce was working all right. Eventually the valley that we hiked along narrowed, and the trail became steeper as we neared the heavens. But to get there, it looked like we would have to troop through a rung of Dante's *Inferno*. We stepped across a muddy stream feeding some sparse vegetation and malnourished trees before entering what looked like a jumbled collection of adobe structures bunched together. Ascending a tight corridor in the settlement felt like walking through an abandoned Egyptian Kasbah, especially as I stepped over a mummified cat splayed in the gutter in a clump of grey fur, ivory white teeth grinning through a twisted mouth.

That was about the only grinning that we encountered in town. The few children we saw peeking around their doorframes before being pulled back inside by protective mothers were subdued, not at all enamored by our novelty. Their youth was replaced with hard stares and furrowed brows of suspicion and judgment, at least at first. The small smiles they cracked after the initial staring contest were priceless, though. Earlier, we saw two small girls looking like neglected dolls, their tiny faces smudged with dirt and their clothes in tatters. They couldn't have been more than five years old, but already they had a swagger about them like miniature *Rosy the Riveters* as they washed loads of clothes by hand. Life is unfair. I learned that well in Iraq, but something about the scene touched a chord in my heart. While other kids their age carelessly bumbled around playgrounds, visited the zoo and had time to be creative, these kids were getting a PhD in survival, in adulthood, in toughness, before most kids in America learned to ride a bike.

The town was depressing and cold, literally. As the sun set lower in the sky, a chill sank into the alleyways like a Passover spirit. We walked further into Jharkot and came upon a weathered looking stupa anointed with a fresh yak head looking down on us like the town's own morbid Walmart greeter. We continued past a row of prayer wheels and made way for a donkey train while Paras and Niraj asked around for a good guest house to bed down in before the Muktinath approach the next day. We would need our rest to make it to the sacred temple and back down towards Jomsom the same day, hopefully making up some lost time. The moment we stopped, my stomach began growling, letting me know that we needed to find a guest house – and *fast*.

The guys found a place with a nice view of the approach to Muktinath and Thorong-La, a high altitude pass located at 5,416 meters (17,769 feet) above sea level, the highest point on the Annapurna Circuit. *Guest house* is a loose term. For a young trekking group, they have only the essentials: a place to sleep, some food, and facilities, if you're lucky. These are definitely not on the Club Med website. They're a hybrid between an elderly person's house and a garage, and while Spartan, make up for their austerity with the hospitality and charm of the innkeepers. In this house, the kitchen doubled as the reception. Heavy smoke billowed out of the room, smelling like a mix of burning shit and diesel fuel. Coughing as we went in, we came across a wind-burnt man in a Pittsburgh Steelers toboggan squatting over an oven, stuffing in fresh limbs with the leaves still on them. With watering eyes, we quickly got our keys and headed up to the room smelling like a trash fire. The musty smell reminded me of the putrid odor of burning shit and plastic in the fire pits on our bases in Baghdad. As I would later learn, a lot of the developing world smells like this. Sojourn – the scent of adventure! I wonder why Ralph Lauren hasn't bottled up this smell for the hipster market yet?

The drill was the same each time we arrived at a hotel room: I dropped dead, face down on the bed, half-sleeping while Nora went about organizing things and freshening up. This time, though, I went straight for the toilet and promptly did my business. As expected, I was relieved of an incredible amount of liquids with some unpleasant after-effects. I had the shits…bad. The good news was that they were controllable for now. The bad news was…the toilet wouldn't flush. The thing was broke! Nauseated by the smoke, and now the malfunction, both mechanical and biological, I reluctantly told the guys that our room needed some special attention. We all left for a stroll, and when we returned to take ice cold showers, the problem was solved. Just the thought of what they had to do to repair the problem triggered a gag reflex, but even worse, I was ridden with guilt for a few minutes at the mess I had caused. Sure, it was their fault the toilet didn't work, but my offense was far worse than theirs, in my opinion.

The cool afternoon turned into an arctic evening, with us pulling out our mountaineering jackets and thick socks to watch the sun cast a fiery red glow over the Annapurna peaks. We went from sweating profusely on the trail to shivering in the chill, plumes of vapor billowing from our mouths and heads in the growing darkness. Before retiring for the night, Nora and I nibbled on Nepalese-style pizzas, which were remarkably faithful reproductions of the Italian versions, considering the poverty and logistical challenges here. Taking careful, small bites, hoping not to awaken the stowaway parasites within us, we nursed some Coca-Cola to settle our stomachs. It was bottled and sealed. We were taking no chances. My adventurous palette lost its appetite for all things exotic and vaguely prepared for the time being. I was going to be a shameless tourist at the dinner table.

The guys were in much better shape than we were. Nora and I were exhausted, but feeling a sense of calm and well-being that only comes after a hard day's physical work. My headache subsided a bit, but a light-headedness settled in, making me slightly giddy. As we sat around talking that night, I sensed a bond of camaraderie forming among us. Paras and Niraj probably wondered what they were getting into with two violently ill tourists who needed help with their rucksacks on the way up. But, they had to be relieved to see us eating and taking in liquids, albeit with the caution of royal tasters.

jharkot to muktinath
and eklebhatti

This is in Nepal.
There is a Shiva's temple.
The path is difficult.
But if you want Mukti,
If you want Muktinath,
The path will become very easy.
Swami Sivananda, Hindu spiritual leader and Yoga master

Rising early in the frozen morning, we began our final ascent to one of the most holy sites in all of Nepal: the Muktinath temple. For Hindus and Buddhists, visiting this Himalayan temple is similar to visiting Vatican City for Christians or Mecca for Muslims. Having made several pilgrimages to the Vatican, I felt solidarity with the pilgrims trekking in plastic sandals and the wandering *Sadhus*. The Sadhu is a scantily-clad holy person, sometimes with dreadlocks, who has left their worldly life in search of *Mukti*, or liberation. Some walk the mountain paths with little more than sackcloth and ashes or pigment smeared on their intense faces.

75

Some look on Sadhus with a mix of reverence and suspicion. On our way to the temple, we passed a sprawling single-story hostel for holy men that looked like a Wild West general store. It existed to shelter the holy men making their trek to holy sites along the path, and as this site was especially holy, there seemed to be more of them. Early in the morning, dozens of bleary-eyed Sadhus milled about in front of the place and lounged on the steps. While some were certainly legitimate men of the cloth, others seemed to be young loafers freeloading on passing tourists and Nepalese alike. The younger men had healthy skin, shiny black hair, and the trinkets hanging from their bodies seemed less inspired, like a hemp bracelet strap with some beads, and other items such as American college students would buy in Florida on spring break. They were likely on the trail to find themselves while living off of others and smoking ganga, not unlike hippies on the same trails decades earlier. The seasoned Sadhus were remarkable, though.

A genuine Sadhu carries himself differently, his dress tells a story, and his hair is usually a chaotic bundle of dreadlocks. They look more like flora than fauna, walking oaks draped in Spanish moss, their skin more like tree bark, their figures often betraying malnourishment. Despite the sharp stones we encountered along most of our path, the true Sadhus walked barefoot. In the freezing morning temperatures, one could tell which Sadhus were legit and which were inexperienced by how they dressed. Some simply had a small sackcloth on, while others had blankets draped around their shoulders. The older Sadhus seemed focused on the path, on meditation, and not so interested in interacting with tourists and posing for photos as the younger ones. I made it a habit not to take any photos of them without asking, and I preferred not to ask. They were individuals on pilgrimage, not props on a movie set. I had to wonder what was going through their minds. Were they holy, or totally baked from ganga and other substances? Did that make any difference? These primitive wild men, looking like witch doctors, complete with bones and feathers adorning some of them, captured my imagination, but unfortunately, I was not able to have a conversation with one.

The climb out of Jharkot was exhausting. We followed a scree-littered trail uphill, and I sucked down gulp after gulp from my water pouch. Predictably, before leaving for the morning I lost a lot of fluids – once in the morning, once in the evening. That is how it would work for the rest of the trip, and while unhealthy, it made the trip manageable. Otherwise, I would have spent two weeks in Nepal hovering over a hole in the ground. But I was thirstier than usual on this ascent, and the mild headache that developed the day before exploded with a bass drum, pulsing sensation that sent an icepick jab to my cranium each time I took a step. I felt like a coke-head holding his breath under 50 feet of water, running in motion. No matter how much I drank, it wasn't enough. My mouth felt like sandpaper, and my heart rate was ridiculously high, pounding like a rabbit running from a hunting party. And, I was starting to talk nonsense.

I'd never experienced high altitude before. In fact, the highest I had been on solid ground was in Sandia Peak, New Mexico, at a little over 10,000 feet (3,050 meters) as a kid. As we approached Muktinath, we were pushing over 12,000 feet, and I was feeling every inch of it. Lightheaded and talking as if half awake, I felt like I was sleepwalking drunk, and this, combined with an insatiable thirst and painful headache, made me question my fitness. Nature has a way of quickly humbling any illusions you might have about your own physical condition, and this was a prime example. Nora and I talked about climbing Kilimanjaro at one point, but I obviously needed to shed about 20 pounds and work on some cardio before seriously planning a trip like that. What I didn't know was that I would be shedding more weight on this trip than I thought was humanly possible in two weeks.

The guys seemed to be doing fine, and Nora was a trooper as always. Everyone laughed at my self-deprecating humor tinged with half serious remarks about death, and who could have my belongings if I collapsed and died on the spot. It was true, I was in pain, but I was hiding the fact that my fat ass was having some doubts about the ascent. That was something other tourist people think, not seasoned trekkers who've explored the Alps and who've been to more developing countries than Angelina Jolie! Was I the overweight, over-prepared American tourist? It seemed so. I was just one degree away from sporting a fanny pack and wearing white tube socks with my sandals.

I needed all of the supernatural help I could get, the guys probably thought, when they stopped to buy some trinkets from peddlers along the trail to the holy site. At least a dozen women sat along the trail with hand-woven blankets sprawled out, displaying everything from miniature bronze prayer wheels on a stick to fossils and other ancient-looking trinkets. Niraj bought a fistful of medallions hanging from a tiny thread and walked over to us, ceremoniously putting them around our necks like Medals of Honor. It *was* a badge of honor, like the scallop shell symbol on the Way of St. James in Spain, which explained why he bought so many. These little pieces of metal displayed a likeness of the Hindu god Vishnu, preserver of the universe.

"I need to take some of these back with me for my family," Niraj said, grinning while packing the medallions away.

"Coming here is a big honor for us," Paras added. "I think we are the first in our families to make it up here, so this is a big deal."

It seemed like a big enough deal to draw grandmas in nothing but saris and flip flops to more than 12,000 feet skyward (3,800 meters). A steady trickle of these devotees arrived at the holy area for a festival that was taking place at the temple in the coming days. I felt both inspired and ridiculous as I stood looking like a sweaty crack head dropped off in the wilderness as these grannies glided past me. They knowingly smiled as we exchanged *namastes* with hands pressed upwards below the chin. This formality eventually became a pleasure. Being a Catholic, this was like the *Sign of Peace* in our own mass, a gesture that leaves one feeling connected with those around you. I offered a slight bow of the head, both to recognize their seniority and my status as a student in their land. While secular western backpackers looked upon the temples and the pilgrims as colorful curiosities, I felt privileged to enter the temple grounds with Paras and Niraj after a tough ascent.

Muktinath-Chumig Gyatsa, called *Mukti Kshetra* or *Place of Salvation* by the Hindus, and *Chumig Gyatsa* or *Hundred Waters* by the Tibetans, is frequented by Hindus and Tibetan Buddhists year round. It is also home to the Muktinath Temple, one of the most sacred Hindu shrines in the world. The temple's construction began in 1815, initiated by Queen Subarna Prabha of Nepal.

The most commonly used name for the temple, *Muktinath*, is comprised of two separate words. Mukti means *savior*, however it can also be used to mean *nirvana*. Nath means *god* or *master*. Each year thousands of pilgrims trek or fly in by helicopter in search of Moksha, or *freedom*, from the continuous spiritual cycle of birth and rebirth. Many believe that the temple should only be visited after one has attended four other sacred sites, such as the Srirangam Island in southern India, the Tirumala Venkateswara Temple in Andhra Pradesh, the town of Pushkar in Rajasthan, or the town of Srimushnam in Tamil Nadu.

The temple pagoda is relatively small, and it is surrounded by an outer courtyard called a *prakaram*, on which there are 108 bull faces. Each of these faces spouts sacred water. The water moves throughout the complex by a network of 108 individual pipes and is ice cold even in the summer. Each spout represent one of the 108 temples devoted to Vishnu, known collectively as the *Divya Desams*, mentioned by the Tamil Azhvars poet saints in their works. Devotees of the Buddhist and Hindu faith alike gather year round to take sacred baths, even in below-freezing temperatures.

The Buddhist and Hindu faiths both believe in Muktinath Temple as a place on Earth where pilgrims can find the five elements at one site: earth, fire, water, sky and air. An eternal flame is fed by natural gas seeping through the rock.

The holy site is maintained by Tibetan Buddhist nuns who live at a monastery next to the Vishnu temple. A young nun robed in a saffron tunic casually emerged from her simple home and went into the temple grounds as we arrived. The area was unusually green for such a high altitude, with small plant life and even trees, like an oasis in the sky. The guys started a conversation with the nun, who seemed more like a bored village girl as she spoke in detached huffs, occasionally looking up from the ground and glancing off into the distance. After a while, she seemed to enjoy the company and warmed up to the guys, walking us over to the temple house to see the deity. This was something usually reserved for the religious, not western tourists with iPod buds in their ears and mouth breathing, confused drive-by glances at weird monuments to superstition. Perhaps sensing our reverence, she opened the door of the shrine for a private viewing, on the condition that no photos be taken.

I felt a swell of anticipation watching Paras and Niraj as they genuflected and meditated piously with the nun looking on. This experience was just as important and real to them as my first time entering the doors of St. Peter's. I was both amazed and wanted to give them space to absorb the moment, not as tour guides, but as pilgrims. I couldn't make out the deity at first, but the guys motioned for me to come closer. The room was dark and dotted with pigment residue, candle wax, and rice offerings, but then I saw the dull golden sheen of what looked like an alien life form, a death mask from another world. The golden deity was swaddled in cloth with its golden face exposed. While it was an inanimate object, and I don't think anyone there was worshiping the statue per se, I felt a heightened sense of spirituality, awareness, and thanked my God for the opportunity to be halfway around the world at the foot of some of the greatest peaks on the planet. I felt blessed to have the privilege to be with them for this moment. The visit is supposed to bring prosperity, and in a peculiar way, it did. Maybe it was pure coincidence, but something happened on my return home that made me think there was more to Muktinath than just culture.

Venerating the deity was not the only thing on offer for the faithful at the temple. There was a physical rite of passage that separated the devout from the Christmas mass crowd. The wall of 108 fountains pouring ice-cold mountain snowmelt offered a rare opportunity at spiritual rebirth and washing away sins. This was definitely not your fiberglass tub baptismal at the local mega-church. This was more like River Jordan meets the Polar Bear Club. Niraj and Paras looked at each other and didn't hesitate one second as they stripped down to their skivvies and prepared for what must be on the opposite end of the spectrum from walking across hot coals. Niraj went first, stepping across frozen sheets of ice barefoot and calmly strolling under each stream. His composure suggested he was in an enlightened, physically detached state. When he reached the last fountain, for good measure, he scrubbed the water over his body, relishing the moment before slipping and sliding over sheets of ice to casually reclaim his clothes. He emerged a new man, shivering slightly, but with an air of serenity and a slightly higher angle of the chin.

Paras was next to make the ancient act of faith. Much skinnier, he walked barefoot across the frozen sheets of ice, calmly at first under the water. Grimacing slightly with the shock of the liquid ice suddenly pouring over him, he scurried along the fountains alternating between faithful, disciplined composure and upright fetal position, with an embarrassed laugh thrown in. With much less insulation than Niraj, his skinny frame shuddered like a Chihuahua locked outside in a snowstorm when he emerged from the holy waters to dry off. He, too, took on a dignified air of calm satisfaction, of grace, once he put his clothes back on and warmed back up. Then it was my turn.

In an act I still regret to this day, I didn't go full polar bear at Muktinath. I walked along each of the fountains, arms outstretched as if holding a skunk as far away from my body as possible, and occasionally splashed some of the holy water on my head. I was already feeling like I had an Oktoberfest-sized hangover and didn't think covering myself in ice water would be a good idea. It may have provided a near death-like experience, but as I already felt near death, I didn't have much more battery power to spare. But looking back, this attempt to keep dry and conscious may have been overcautious. If women old enough to be my grandma could do it after hiking for days, probably afflicted by their own bowel problems, I should have done it, too. It would have been a shock, though. My hands were completely numb after passing them through the water, so I could only imagine what Niraj and Paras felt like. One thing was certain; our extraordinary nature walk had turned into a strangely satisfying ecumenical experience at 12,000 feet.

Muktinath felt like it was at the top of the world, the last outpost before the pearly gates. Through an ornate red gate in the main garden, you could see the cone-shaped Dhampus Peak in the distance, a massive mountain with thick snow cover. Looking closely at the peaks, you could see violently swirling clouds of snow in the hurricane force winds. Even at over 12,000 feet, jagged peaks and ridgelines towered around us, reaching even higher into the sky. It was hard to believe that human beings conquered peaks like these, and even greater ones like Everest and K2. Nora knew I had illusions of climbing Everest one day, and reading my mind, she reminded me of my sorry state.

"So, Mr. Thompson, you *still* want to climb Mount Everest, huh?" she said.

How does she do that? How could she read my mind exactly in that moment? It's as if she knew that I was coming to grips with what was only a private fantasy. But, she knew well that our crazy ideas were also the seeds of real experiences. This trip was one of them.

"Ugh…well…I dunno, I think…er…I dunnnt wanna do dat anymrr," I said drunk on altitude sickness. She raised an eyebrow, surprised that I didn't put up more resistance to defeat. Just saying the words hurt a bit, and I wasn't sure what I was saying, and what I did say came out slurred. In the temple, I felt enlightened and had a heightened sense of awareness, but the euphoria was wearing off. The truth was…*HELL NO*…did I ever want to climb Everest? What a stupid idea! Apparently, there was enough oxygen to fire some cognitive dissonance reaction in my brain. Seriously, though, the experience was enough to extinguish any remote illusions of ever conquering Everest. Maybe, just maybe, passing the Thorong-La, but not Everest, with my Baghdad trash fire lungs and 20 pounds of residual Western cuisine hanging around my hips. At 12,000 feet, I already felt like I had the cognitive abilities of a praying mantis, and could not possibly imagine going above 20,000 feet. A man has his limits, and it looked like, at least with my office- place physique back then, I had hit my glass ceiling of willpower. Plus, as Nora already knew, climbing Everest would be incredibly stupid when there were more important things in life like being there for my future wife instead of playing Russian roulette.

The call of adventure is a lot like the siren of Homer's *Odyssey*. I recalled a quote about the search for adventure ruining more men than women and drink, and after traveling the globe, I think this is sometimes true. It can become a quest for constant intoxicating disorientation, of exotic vistas, of belonging everywhere and nowhere at once, of shedding the tame life of the suburbs to force the release of suppressed, primal shots of adrenaline once reserved as a natural cocaine to endure mortal combat, childbirth, and outsmart predators. As westerners, many of us have taken on the form and minds of the modern man, but deep within our hearts, we still long for the hunt, for roaming, for the rewards of physical exertion. In a society where actual physical exertion is not only impractical to survival, but also economically disadvantageous, we are wired and built to endure things like Himalayan life and survive the Mekong floods in floating villages – but our minds are now programmed for a different kind of survival, allowing us to become wealthy in virtual realms without breaking a sweat. In this conflict of thinking and living like a modern man, but having the heart of natural man, dreams of adventure are born. This is what I thought as we sat on the balcony of the Bob Marley Café for breakfast while talking to a first-time adventurer.

Frostbite is a sure sign that someone found adventure in Thorong-La. Some may even consider it a badge of honor. Bastiaan wore that badge of honor on conspicuous parts of his face. The young Dutchman just descended the path from Thorong-La and past Muktinath when we noticed him sitting at a table next to ours at a café vaguely reminiscent of a rickety bait and tackle shop in the bayou. He seemed cheery and alert as he thumbed absentmindedly through a travel guide and took in the sunshine, but after exchanging a few words, his cheery absentmindedness seemed more like nervousness, with some visible wincing when he thought no one was looking.

"Hey man, so did you just come down from the pass?" Niraj asked.

"Oh, yes…it was very difficult, yes…" he replied while "Redemption Song" played in the background. "A little painful, I think, but very good…" he said, almost as much to convince himself as to keep in the conversation.

"What is that on your face? Doesn't look good man."

"Ah, yes, I think I may have a small problem. This frostbite is on my face, I think."

"Man, you should have that looked at somewhere," Niraj said.

"Yes, yes, this is a good idea. But I don't know where. We are so far away, so I say, whatever! Just relax like Bob Marley. My friends are sleeping now, so I wait on them and we get help later."

"What was it like going through the pass?" I asked.

"Really incredible. We were up at midnight to walk through. It was like we were on another planet. But honestly, I did not see much. It was very dark," he said like a war veteran. "It was very windy and we kept very close through the pass. It was hard work, and there were some problems, people not ready," he said while touching his sores.

"Some people did not have the proper clothes, no," he went on. "They brought an Israeli girl down who was hiking in house shoes and panicked. What do they think, this is a vacation?" not realizing the irony of telling this story through his own frostbite-blotched mouth.

"I don't know, this is my first time really outside of Holland, and we don't have mountains, so this was a big surprise. My friends told me this would be adventurous and they have done things like this before, but I am not so sure. I think I am ready to go home now."

We were also ready to head home, to Jomsom. We planned on backtracking to the town and taking advantage of downhill trekking speed, continuing on the Annapurna Circuit to the lowlands over several days. Already losing one day to sickness, we needed to keep a brisk pace if we were going to make it to civilization in time to catch a bus back to Kathmandu. The only way to do that after passing the Jomsom airstrip was in Beni, about 40 miles (65 kilometers) away, through rough terrain. High winds, high temperatures, and precipitation all meant this wouldn't be a walk in the park, even if it were downhill.

The trek downhill was brisk and mostly quiet across terrain we were already familiar with. The deep canyon we hiked along seemed like something out of *Star Wars*. I was cherishing the views, holding on to each moment, knowing I may never return, taking mental snapshots and thanking God for each moment, knowing how special this was. There is something in the air in Nepal, an ambience that seems to emanate from the elements. Nature inspired inner peace, but the people inspired a sense of community too. It wasn't just their hospitality. Other countries had hospitable people. There was something uniquely different here. Was it their innocence in a globalized world, their conspicuous humility? Whatever it was, the Nepali people were genuinely friendly, with none of the "my friend!" antics that usually meant the exact opposite in other countries. Nepal is genuine, it's spiritual. While the country may be rather poor, it is unmistakably rich in faith and spirit.

My thoughts turned more spiritual during the trek too. The act of walking created a rhythm that aligned physical exertion with mental awareness, making the physical activity like a prayer. Each strike of the heel created a rhythm like fingers passing over rosary beads, a prayerful clockwork of mind and body, synchronizing and becoming more aware of space and time. It was as if the act of walking and being aware of God in nature combined to form an unspoken prayer. Under a brilliant, deep blue sky lined with majestic peaks, thoughts were unlocked, questions were asked, and God felt near. What was I supposed to learn on this trip? Would I ever return here? Why do many in our western civilization deny God? Why do some see God as the problem, as a primitive notion? Cannot modern society and God coexist? Of course, they do in many ways still, but out here on the trail, I wondered how we could even hear the voice of God, much less our own thoughts and deep feelings, over the noise of modern society. I realized that this was a reason I liked coming to the developing world: there was still a deep reverence for God, in many forms, and I felt a strong sense of solidarity with people like that, whether they were Iraqi friends who pressed on with life optimistically despite the dangers they were in, or an Egyptian shopkeeper who took us to a neighborhood for dinner and discussed the meaning of life while we sat on a shop floor, or the old women in saris walking dozens of miles uphill in flip flops because of their faith. Some might argue that is why some of these countries are poor and dysfunctional, because they are superstitious, lacking a protestant work ethic, too naïve to learn how to structure their lives and become productive.

The Maoist insurgents in Nepal, who suppressed religious freedom, had their own answers. We passed a shelter resembling an Afghani adobe structure, and I noticed a sun-bleached poster plastered to the side. A hammer and sickle logo emanated holy rays along with an iconic, almost religious-like portrait of Prachanda. The designer clearly spent some time at the Kim Jung-Il School of Industrial Art. Prachanda had been leading a vicious guerilla war in the former kingdom of Nepal since 1995, but was seeking a legitimate government seat. He had just signed a peace agreement with Kathmandu in November 2006, a few months before our arrival. I knew there was a Maoist insurgency in Nepal for years, but had no idea it claimed approximately 15,000 lives in a little over 10 years. We couldn't have chosen a better time to visit.. According to the guys, the situation was very complicated, but there was a general peace at the moment. The poster called for support of Prachanda's agenda and his election into the government, where they would try to peacefully reform the government, abolish the monarchy, and redistribute wealth to the peasants, who were mostly working agricultural jobs for scraps. One thing was for sure, with its tough geography and limited industrialization, it was going to take more than Maoism to get Nepal on the path to solid development. In long talks with Niraj and Paras, it didn't seem that the country lacked the willpower and brainpower to create a better future. The two of them were just as clever as their counterparts in the developed world.

Despite our collective cleverness, we lost the trail somehow. The land's texture was so windswept and monotonous that the trail lines would fade in and out of view. With no trail markers, and no one around for miles, we continued to descend towards the village of Kagbeni. The village sits at the gateway of the deep Upper Mustang region bordering on China and serves as a way-station for trekkers heading north into the exotic region. Access carried an exotic price tag, too. A week of hiking in the Upper Mustang cost a western trekker over $700, which explained why it wasn't on our itinerary. The Kagbeni Yak Donald's restaurant was within budget, but by the look of the cliff we were approaching, entering Kagbeni was out of the question, as was finding a good trail. It was around this time that I noticed the "motion prayer" clearly produced a useful phenomenon. The cadence of the prayer created momentum like a tailwind that would push us along dangerous trails, taking risks that I would not have normally taken back home. I began to sense this momentum just as winds began to rush down the peaks into the canyons, buffeting our ears and kicking up dust.

Niraj and Paras were not yet professional guides, but by the look of things, they were off to a promising start. Even with two sick westerners, an itinerary we threw at them at the last minute, and no experience in the remote region, they made sure we were airlifted, well-medicated, hydrated, fed, and bedded down as if they were Nepal's number one travel experts. Standing on the edge of the cliff overlooking Yak Donald's hometown, they decided to abort our attempt to reach the Kali Gandaki river bed and instead planned to skirt the edge of the canyon along an unprepared stretch. It was too late to backtrack and find the main trail. With the sun already sitting lower on the horizon and winds picking up rapidly, overland was our only option. Nora and I bit our tongues. We weren't exactly lost, because we had good maps and could guess where we were, but we were going to lose some time.

The path was rougher than expected, with sheer drops along the way. For some reason, despite being a pilot, I developed a queasiness about heights sometime between youth and now. I definitely wouldn't be a good candidate for one of those outdoor gear advertisements of a decked-out, perfectly kempt adventurer standing on the tippy top of a peak with arms upstretched in victory. No, I would be cautiously crawling, stretched spread-eagle across the peak, hugging it for dear life with several redundant systems to ensure I didn't fall off somehow. Not that I was ashamed. Most of those North Face fellas in the ads were probably dropped off by a helicopter anyway!

Nora seemed oblivious to most natural dangers in general. I've seen her navigate the Alps like a mountain goat, taking hefty risks, only to turn around as if to ask, "Are we there yet?" That, and stepping casually over a poisonous snake in the Ardeche of southern France. As a Frankfurt city girl, she said she didn't know it was dangerous.

With the momentum of the cadence of the physical prayer, things like heights didn't seem to bother me anymore. What did bother me was the surface of our path. Up until now, the trails were smooth, with a few simple water crossings. Now we stumbled along an unstable canyon ledge on a wild path covered in sharp stones the size of cantaloupes. This caused each boot strike to wobble, threatening to roll an ankle. With the arches of my feet already feeling like they were being pounded by a rubber mallet, this was an unwelcome nature walk. The rocks were perfect for ruining a stride. Any smaller and you could simply find two points of contact for a pretty level step. Any larger, and you could walk and hop along the tops. But these rocks were pointy and unstable, and this went on for miles and miles. Any serenity I experienced up in the hills faded away as I pursed my lips, and a silence descended on the usual hiking banter. The guys knew we were on the trail from hell and were probably embarrassed that we had ended up there. I sympathized but didn't feel like talking until we were back on *terra firma*. Paras was probably thinking the same thing and stayed behind, taking a private smoke break overlooking the valley and the sun casting long shadows below. I didn't know at the time there would be an even worse trail later.

We weren't going to make it to Jomsom on time. Our detour was too time-consuming, but there was an upside. Now, our overnights would be staggered at smaller towns along the route instead of the main tourist stopovers. That would give us a better sense of rural Nepal instead of being holed up in backpacker hostels. Eklebhatti would be home for the night, the guys signaled, emerging from an isolated lodge with a thumbs up. Nora coached me up off a stone wall where I lay, mouth agape, my rucksack still on like a tranquilized camel. After a tough day, we were finally going to rest.

The friendly lodge owners quickly showed us to our rooms, perhaps sensing that I was going to pass out at any moment. A woman led us into the timber structure, through the central grand room that stretched to the roof, surrounded by second floor railing and up a rickety staircase. Opening the door of the room, she looked at us for approval. The place was immaculate, in a timbered Tibetan monetary sense. Sure, pretentious, overpriced *McRooms* in places like D.C. may have a nice brand name on them, but they are often clean and lacking any sense of character. This place had character and cleanliness in the middle of nowhere. I wanted to give the didi a hug, but she quickly left with a big smile to prepare the evening's meal. Nora and I commenced our usual ritual. Being a lady, she would predictably inspect the room and offer some commentary about the cleanliness, quality of bedding, and bathroom facilities. I offered approving grunts while laying like a wet towel on a driveway, face down in the bed drooling on myself. I faded in and out of consciousness, with the darkness behind my eyelids enveloping my mind like a dense opiate cloud. I was so exhausted that rest was actually making me high.

"These blankets are so hard," Nora reported while holding up a shabby carpet covering the mattress.

I began laughing deliriously, and she soon followed. "Waa'r yer talkin' 'bout? Dad's a carpet!" I said exhausted and half dreaming.

"What are you talking about? How am I supposed to sleep under this?" she asked, laughing while miming covering herself in the stiff cloth.

"Izza cover. Ya sleep on top of it, I think," I replied.

"Okay! I knew that, I was just kidding with you. Now get up! I'm hungry!" she said while jumping in the shower, reporting that the pressure and temperature were acceptable. I don't know where she was getting her energy from. I spent months, if not well over a year collectively on military maneuvers, and in Iraq and Kuwait living like a stray dog, and I never remembered being this tired before. As I was wondering if this is what it felt like to get old, my parasite reminded me it was time to make more room for him. I suddenly jumped out of bed, tripping over myself to get to the toilet. The truth was that my body was under an incredible amount of stress from the parasite alone. I wasn't vomiting anymore, but my twice-daily bowel movements, while now somewhat tamed and predictable, were disturbing in magnitude. It was about this time I noticed my pants fitting looser than ever.

Late evening in the lodge reminded me of Marion's tavern in the Nepal scene of Indiana Jones from *Raiders of the Lost Ark*. We sat with the guys down in the grand room and ate a dinner of porridge, mashed potatoes, and pizza à la Nepal, all of which were surprisingly good. For being on the frontier, the lodge keepers could cook up a worldly meal better than most people. Not to mention that most of their goods were brought in on donkey trains or on the backs of mountain men. We all sat around and joked about the detour, which seemed less inconvenient now and maybe even a blessing in disguise, now that we would be staying at smaller villages for the remainder of the trek.

As we sat in the grand room, the husband and wife innkeepers distanced themselves at another table to enjoy each other's company. As the husband sipped a hot tea, his wife went over to an antique cabinet. Surely it was an heirloom piece passed down by those proud-looking parents, immortalized in slightly out of focus black and white portraits looking down on us from the banister. It probably contained items worthy of display in the Smithsonian, maybe rare trinkets from the abandoned monastic caves in the Mustang, or rare shaligrams. A whiff of incense caught my imagination as she carefully opened the treasure chest.

Apparently, Nepalese value home entertainment systems as much as Americans do. Didi opened the cabinet to reveal cultural treasures of another kind: a big screen color television and satellite receiver! Like two lovebirds cuddled in a movie theater, they sat and enjoyed their meal while flipping to a British sports channel featuring darts. Apparently, this was mesmerizing stuff, because they unblinkingly watched every move beamed out of the English coal country tavern. Pasty-skinned, intense-looking Englishmen in crew cuts tossed darts half a world away in the working class North country while entertaining another kind of working class North country folk perched at the top of the world near Tibet. *Globalization had arrived in Eklebhatti,* I thought to myself as the two nodded approvingly at the best tosses. That night, I fell asleep like a little kid, hearing the low din of an English sports announcer's unintelligible babble echoing through the house as our adopted parents enjoyed date night in the middle of nowhere in the Himalayas.

eklebhatti to tukche

We stepped out into the cool morning air in the shadow of the mountains to continue our trek. The valley was still dark, but the mountain peaks surrounding us were already a brilliant white. With many of the peaks reaching over 18,000 feet (5,400 meters), they captured the sun's rays over the horizon well before anything at ground level did. In this Tibetan climate region, cool morning temperatures quickly became hot in direct sunlight, searing the skin at a faster rate than at sea level. The dry, dusty wind chafed the skin, wicking away moisture, but in the calm morning air, the atmosphere was peaceful and filled the lungs with refreshing cool air. At this altitude, about 9,000 feet (2,900 meters), altitude sickness wasn't a problem. I noticed some aches, though.

For me, hiking has a discomfort bell curve. If I haven't been training, which was the case for Nepal, walking for hours day after day twisted and turned my muscles and tendons to where every part of my body felt like I was being beaten with a broomstick. Especially irritable were my shoulders, where my rucksack straps shifted thousands of times a day. Like rubbing two sticks together, this generated heat and soreness before I learned to shift the weight from my shoulders to my hips by strapping the kidney pads tightly above my hipbone. While this may seem like common sense, getting the technique right took time, and the reader is well advised to do some research about rucksack settings before heading out on a multiday hike, especially with a heavy load. I was most worried about my feet, though.

My feet have not been the most reliable mode of transportation in the past. When I was younger, they swelled after long periods of standing, where I found it nearly impossible to stay upright. My ankles swelled like balloons and become soft to the touch like overripe peaches. In Army basic training, this painful phenomenon began about two weeks into the program of standing in formation for hours at a time, at attention, learning the art of discipline. I simultaneously learned the art of suppressing excruciating pain. When I confided in my bunkmate that I had a case of the chorizo ankles, he recoiled.

"Whaaaaaat the fuuuuuuck" he said. "Man, I would get that checked out. I don't want you dying on me."

But I didn't want to get kicked out on a medical, either. I didn't want to be like the overweight guy made to stand out in the barracks courtyard forced to suck his thumb and yell, "Wah, wah! I want my mommy! I want my milk and cookies!" for hours until lights out. I wouldn't be falling out. I had nowhere to go if I did, so I got hold of some Ace bandages and wrapped my lower leg as tight as I could, and laced my boots with enough force to choke a crocodile. Medical professionals reading this are probably cringing, but somehow it worked. I was able to make it through training with flying colors, and the fluid in my ankles eventually displaced and disappeared. I knew, though, that my feet were ticking time bombs. It was years since I had a problem with them, but then again, I hadn't pushed them to these limits in recent years.

I kept careful watch over my feet. With breathable German hiking boots, arch supports, and form-fitting socks, they seemed pretty secure. I had a full blister kit of tough adhesive silicone skin, moleskin, needles, and disinfectant. I learned to rub small amounts of Vaseline between my toes to reduce friction, which seemed to help. Surprisingly, the walk along the "trail from hell" the day earlier seemed to relieve my ankles by rotating them constantly. It felt like the pain curve was about as bad as it was going to get, and from here out, my body would respond with strength instead of weakness.

We walked along the Kali Gandaki riverbed, back-tracking our earlier route to Jomsom, passing a pair of wild horses along the banks. They screeched at each other on their hind legs. With wild white eyes popping out of their heads, they punched at each other like kangaroos and bit at each other's necks. We paused from a safe distance as they battled for the nearby mares. I'd never seen anything like it, and didn't even know horses could be so aggressive. It was like suddenly learning that Mr. Ed was a gangster by night. I was awestruck and cautious at the same time. I didn't want their wild eyes turning to us and coming after us with their flailing hooves like the horse in the movie at the airport in Pokhara. Eventually, the weaker horse decided he'd had enough and galloped away, shaking off the blows. We pushed on and noticed the smell of burning wood hanging heavy in the morning air.

While condors carried away the dead in the higher elevations, riverside funeral pyres were the norm in the lower elevations. Walking into the Jomsom town limits, we noticed a group of villagers standing around a pile of wood in the riverbed. I raised my camera to get a shot of the riverside family reunion, but suddenly stopped.

"Dan, no man," Niraj said quickly when he saw me prepare for the shot. "That is a funeral, man. We have to respect the dead."

"Yeah, they will be upset if they see you doing that," Paras added. "We have to respect the culture. This is a very holy ceremony."

We stood on a suspension bridge and watched as smoke poured out across the valley. The ashes would be placed into the holy Gandaki waters and find their way eventually to the holiest river in Hinduism, the Ganges. The Gandaki is a major tributary of the legendary river, carrying waters from Tibet and Nepal to the lowlands, into India and the Bay of Bengal. Hindus believe that placing the ashes in the holy waters brings the person closer to nirvana.

I felt relatively closer to nirvana as we stopped at our former guesthouse in Jomsom for a quick bite of fried Tibetan bread and wild honey with the friendly didi. Compared to my pitiful state when we first came to Jomsom, I felt much better and taking on more fluids. There were still complications, but I learned to live with them. On our way out of town, a young policeman thumbed attentively through our paperwork and logged us into a book. They tracked our movements just in case we went missing along the way. At some later checkpoints, I noticed these weren't simply information centers for tourists, but reinforced military checkpoints protecting lines of communication, presumably under threat from Maoists. There was a peace agreement now, but with the ink not yet dry, the government didn't seem to be letting its guard down.

We weren't letting our guard down when it came to fluids, either. As much as I wanted to enjoy the butter tea, I limited myself to bottled water, cola, the occasional beer, and lots of Tang. At these remote places, this created a burden on the environment. Full bottles of everything were in high demand, enough that a steady stream of goods came in non-stop on the backs of donkeys and men. The only problem was that empty containers were worthless, sometimes littering the countryside. Everything that was carried in would need to be carried out again.

A New Zealand NGO came up with a novel solution. They installed ozone filter systems at strategic spots along the Annapurna Circuit, offering pure drinking water. It provided some jobs, safe water, and reduced the plastic bottle litter problem. For a few cents, we filled up our empty bottles and Camelbak water pouches with parasite-free refreshment...at least I hoped so. Staying hydrated became more important as we left the dry Tibetan climate for a temperate climate zone.

Our next stop would be the village of Marpha. On the way there, we passed a singular house with a street-wise little boy looking us up and down. His plump features and hustler swagger should have warned us immediately.

"Give me money," he said.

"I don't have any money," I said, used to this kind of conversation after 14 months in Iraq. I knew it was hard to say no, but supporting begging just made things worse in nearly every case.

"You give me money. Money now." He definitely wasn't a poster boy for the Nepal Tourism Board.

The pint-sized panhandler curled his lip as we turned our backs and continued on. Suddenly, with the speed of a mongoose in a cobra fight, his hand shot into Nora's pants pocket before recoiling back to the house empty-handed. He took a chance, but luckily her pockets were empty. Nora was visibly shaken by the encounter with the miniature mugger. The guys immediately trailed him to the house and reported him to his mom. That was no way to be treating guests, they explained.

The landscape was rapidly changing from a monotonous desert-like adobe and gravel color to rich brown and green patches of young barley. There were even a few solitary trees, some blossoming with pink flowers. The blooming apple trees contrasted beautifully with the blue sky. We stopped at a row of meticulously maintained white stupas and prayer wheels along the road with a group of pilgrims headed north. Pausing to pray at the site, they continued on, cluttered like newcomers to Ellis Island in the back of a trailer pulled by a dilapidated tractor. It was only motorized public transportation system in these parts, it seemed. We inspected the site, and I noticed large, flat stones inscribed with Sanskrit piled around the holy site. They were mantras, dozens of them, like Rosetta Stones from an ancient past. Later, I would develop an eye for these prayer tablets sitting along the trail, which looked like ordinary rocks until the sunlight reflected floral patterns and prayers that looked a thousand years old. Like many things on this trail, it was not enough to simply walk it. You had to be aware of it, eyes ever scanning, mindful of the details, open to contact with the people. Otherwise, it would just be a nature hike, a blur, a nice picture passing by to go along with the iPod playlist.

Marpha was the first green village on our tour so far. With a few evergreen trees, waist-high barley waving in the wind, and apple orchards, the place wasn't bone dry like Jomsom and Jharkot. We made our way through the narrow alleyways of the town dotted with simple tourist cafés in buildings of whitewashed stone. Tattered prayer flags fluttered wildly, contrasting with the white buildings and piles of wood stacked neatly on the rooftops. Winds picked up, as they did every midmorning, so we decided to take some refuge and get a proper bite to eat past the town at an orchard hostel. I was becoming bolder, wanting to evolve from my diet of mashed potatoes and cheese with Coca Cola. This morning, I ordered an omelet, a risky move. Despite my noxious *eggy* burps earlier in Pokhara, I was craving a real breakfast. Potatoes and fried dough weren't going to offer me enough nourishment if I wanted to regain my strength, especially with Mother Nature turning the thermostat up. I needed to start eating vitamins.

The lodge sat nestled within a lush tree plantation. Business was booming, according to a charismatic local man who joined us in the gazebo over breakfast. He was the apparent owner.

"I am vurry fust appl'a farmer een Marpha," Johnny Appleseed of the Annapurna said, leaning back proudly. "I am also inveent the appl wiz-keee. I am vury famous, yes," he continued while passing out dried apple chips.

I nibbled on them carefully, not wanting to overload my stomach. I needed to ease it back into normal operation, if that was at all possible.

"I am take the Marpha appl' and make famous in the Europe and the USA, yes."

We all nodded as he went on to explain the varieties of apple products he'd invented and made famous, like a Nepali version of Benjamin Buford "Bubba" Blue in *Forrest Gump*, telling Forrest all the ways he could prepare shrimp. We continued to nod, sinking our teeth into hot apple pancakes and surprisingly good omelets. Receiving some foreign aid and technical assistance, the town was developing beyond trail tourism into organic fruit farming, producing apples and apple wine, among other things. It was a modest attempt to diversify beyond grains and trekking commerce. From the look of things, the plan was working relatively well. I cautiously sipped some water mixed with Tang, growing anxious to hit the trail again and leave Johnny Appleseed.

In this lower climate region, nature's own colors slowly bled into the landscape. At higher elevations, the only vibrant colors were prayer flags and decorations, but beginning in Marpha, wildflowers, tree blossoms, and barley fields all created a Garden of Eden feel compared to the bone dry landscape we experienced earlier. The austere highlands produced a natural ascetical dimension, nature's monastery made of weathered rock, encircled by icy watchtowers and devoid of sound, as if in low earth orbit. Here in the lowlands, the landscape increasingly showed signs of life, of worldly routine, of fertility.

We continued our trek along the awesome Kali Gandaki valley, the vast riverbed like a gash in the surface of the earth. Like a massive mirror, sunlight reflected from the packed snow high above us with blinding white light. The ridgeline was an all-star lineup of famous, or infamous, peaks. The Dhaulagiri I climbed an impossible 26,794 feet (8,166 meters) into the sky, while to our left, the Nilgiri spewed snow mist like an ice volcano at 23,166 feet (7,069 meters). Further, beyond the horizon, stood the Nilgiri South peak at 22,437 feet (6,838 meters). The scene was awe-inspiring, a reminder of how small we are as a people, how incredibly powerful the forces of the earth are, how our lifetimes are but nanoseconds on this majestic rock spinning in the black coldness of outer space.

More than ever, the trail became a meditation. Each of us grew quiet at this point, and the small talk slowed to a trickle. We weren't tiring of each other's company. There was no selfish desire for mental distance. It was something different. The Annapurna Circuit in itself was a fantastic nature walk, but as an experience, it was like a linear prayer medium, like a rosary or aisle in a majestic house of worship. The visual landscape enveloped me in beauty, producing a healing balm for the interior mind. The occasional whiff of incense and exchanging of *namaste* blessings with passing grandmothers conjured a mixed feeling of mysticism and community. As before, my boots pressing against this ancient land and my body lurching forward with each step, blissfully clutching my rucksack straps against my aching body, created a cadence that aligned body, mind, and spirit in a perfect trinity of awareness. This was the essence of pilgrimage the world over, be it on the Way of Saint James, Muktinath, or Mecca. In this transfixed state, each of us retreated into the attics of our minds, opening long-forgotten dusty boxes of memories and illuminating darker areas with the enlightenment of the experience around us. We found new feelings, revelations, and wisdom that were all but impossible to unlock with the sensory overload of routine life, of fleeting moments of clarity in between work and relaxation where it could be salvaged. The Annapurna Circuit was taking a hold on us.

"AMERICA...FUCK YEAHHHH! COMING TO SAVE THE MUTHA FUCKIN' DAY, YEAHHHH!" came echoing through the valley behind us, breaking the sound of gravel beneath our feet like a fart in church. An athletic-looking American we'd occasionally seen along the way since Jharkot and his Nepali guide burst into laughter singing this song over and over again. I was annoyed at first, but then chuckled at the song. The American was dragging his poles and it looked like the trail was getting the best of him. His guide, a hip, younger Nepali decked out in the latest North Face gear, conversed with him in clichéd English phrases learned from pirated American movies. Paras and Niraj were reading my mind when they suggested we slow down to let them pass us. As they did, I noticed the American had ear-buds plugged into his ears and an iPod strapped to his chest.

I love music, and especially love listening to music while traveling. Creating a soundtrack to life has always added some spice to otherwise dull moments. It can charm a bit of introspection from my thoughts like a cobra out of a basket in a Moroccan market. Today, I carry an iPod almost wherever I go, never missing an opportunity to fill my head with tunes or a good podcast. But back then, I remember feeling sorry for the guy. The device was almost contaminating, like a hypodermic needle washing up on the shore or a leaky oil drum in the forest. How could you ever replace the sounds of the Himalayas, the *namastes*, the howling wind, the donkey train bells, the throaty Om Mani Padme Hum mantra echoing from open doors and windows in the villages – with Eminem? How could you listen to your heart? How could you follow the whispers of your inner curiosity, of nature?

There were a lot of dusty boxes and new thoughts in the attic of my mind to go through once Team America passed us, and soon we were back in our meditative state. Where was my life taking me? Was I making the right decision working in Germany as an editor for a magazine, taking courses online instead of throwing caution to the wind and becoming a full resident at a university in the States? Was I limiting myself? Did I lack the courage to go into free fall and start my own business? What did I want to be, to become? The truth was, I was still finding my way after experiencing Iraq. Suddenly, the world was much bigger and much more accessible. I wanted to know more about the world, and find my place in making it better. I knew I would never be able to accomplish that as an editor working for the Army. Yes, I could make an impact in a small way – but not in a way time demands of someone who almost has their life taken from them, as mine almost was in Iraq…twice that I knew of. Right when I thought I knew about the world, Iraq happened, and suddenly, a gate was swung open to a vast new world – a gate as wide as the Kali Gandaki valley. I wanted to know more about it. I wanted to know the people living beyond my world, to learn their stories. I wanted this because the more I learned about the world, the more I learned about myself, the more I valued my freedoms, and the more I realized heaven is perhaps not some distant oasis in the sky: It is right here on earth. It was full of good people in every place we discovered, many of them with the same hopes and fears as my own.

Iraq was very much on my mind. Perhaps it was the smell of burning trash or diesel exhaust. Perhaps it was the poverty and the wide-eyed glances from skinny children. Whatever it was, I was still making peace with my experiences there. Something positive was born out of that wartime experience, and this trek was just an example. The day I learned I was being deployed to Iraq, I felt like I was standing before the guillotine of fate, before the precipice of destruction. My world, centered around Nora, suddenly shattered as I tried to clutch the shards to my chest and pray that it was all a bad dream. I remembered the promise made to me in an alcove of St. Peter's by an Italian priest at the Vatican, hearing my pre-deployment confession: "Protect your life, and protect the lives of the innocent while in Iraq, and you will be granted protection. Go and be an instrument of peace." Four years later, Nora and I were in the Himalayas, safe and sound, with two Nepalese who were becoming our good friends. Experiences like this made me realize that evil, like the bestial evil witnessed in Iraq, and the kind that afflicted many parts of the world, could be conquered by good. I learned that the world was full of people just like me and Nora who cared about their freedom, about the necessity to work hard for change, to work together to solve problems. With each trip, with each adventure, my faith in people was reaffirmed in a real and personal way. Nora, Paras, and Niraj were all having their own deep thoughts. Some of those thoughts discovered on the trail during this special time were the seeds of greater things to come for all of us, things that may not have come to pass if we hadn't headed into the unknown.

Picking lodgings for the night along the Annapurna Circuit, you have to be open-minded. For example, if hot water and clean sheets are a must, then you would be better off visiting Orlando, Florida than planning a trip to Nepal. However, upon our arrival in the rustic village of Tukche, Paras and Niraj scouted a fine lodge run by a Dutchman and his Nepali wife. As Nora and I waited outside resting our backs against a wall, a troop of at least 30 French tourists shuffled into town, cameras in hand. It was unusual to see such a large group of tourists, and as we hoped they would continue, their Nepali guide decided to push on to the next village. I sighed a breath of relief, wanting the entire guesthouse to ourselves, without having to worry about any late-night, alcohol-induced talent contests echoing through the building while I slept. Although, I was invariably subdued by the end of each day, and could have slept through a violent earthquake, much less a group of Frenchmen being herded from place to place like timid sheep.

"We're good!" Paras emerged from the guesthouse with the good news. We would be able to spend the night there, and we were early enough to enjoy some activities before retiring for the night. Nora and I entered the stairwell to our room and bumped along the sides of the hallway with our over-packed rucksacks throwing our balance off just before the most anxious moment of every night – opening the door to our room. What secrets (or bugs) lurked within? What type of bedding would we have (with or without dog scent)? How much would the room smell like the auxiliary chimney?

"Wow, look at this!" Nora said after opening the door and stepping inside. Indeed, we seemed to have stepped into a Swiss chalet! The light wood paneling and attention to detail to the bedding looked as good as any ski lodge in Europe. There were distinctly Nepali accents as well, from the colorful lamps to the textiles used. After spending the night in some tolerable, nonetheless rustic, cabins, it was nice to have higher-than-average lodgings for one night. Whereas I could sleep on cardboard in a gutter and be fine, Nora was understandably less tolerant of unnecessary poverty and visibly happy to have a comfortable and familiar place to recover.

After laying somewhat comatose in my superior bed while Nora showered in a gleaming bathroom, I summoned the willpower to peel my aching, lazy body from the infinite comfort of the crisp white sheets and take a shower myself. After all, the sun was still shining and I had the distinct feeling that loafing on such an afternoon would be a complete waste. It was our first warm shower of the trip, and it was luxurious. I had felt unusually drained in the evenings, despite my strength during the day. I was sure that the diarrhea I had resigned myself to cooperating with twice a day was tremendously draining my energy. However, it was only once in the morning and again in the afternoon when nature would come calling, albeit fiercely, giving me the better part of the day without any digestive terror. As I have with many terrors, I use humor to deal with it.

Stepping under the shower, I was overcome by the pure bliss of hot water covering my body, and slipped into a fit of giddiness. Perhaps needing to hear Nora laugh as she preoccupied herself with organizing for the evening, or needing to vent some self-deprecating humor to relieve my anxiety about carrying a condition that could send me running for the bushes at any moment, I began to hum a little ode to my ailment.

Because I chose to eat
Raw buffalo meat
I got a parasite!

Now there's hookworms in my stool
And there's nothin' I can do

Because I chose to eat
Raw buffalo meat
I got a parasite!

Now I've got the nasty runs
And it really ain't no fun

Because I chose to eat
Raw buffalo meat
I got a parasite!

As with many of my lunatic tunes, I went on to amuse Nora for at least another four verses, which regrettably have escaped my memory. But for the moment, we were falling over ourselves, laughing hysterically at my hit song.

"Dan made a song about his little friend," Nora said as we sat down with Niraj and Paras on the porch of the lodge along the village corridor. Nora began using the word "friend" to describe what we guessed at the time was giardia, a parasite commonly found in dogs that produces revolting *eggy* burps and turns intestines into water balloons, in constant danger of bursting like a child's toy. It had taken on a persona, like an unborn child, and I was its pregnant mother.

Somewhat embarrassed at our private moment turned public, I reluctantly shared a few verses with our friends, not sure the humor would translate well – especially before dinner. Of course, the song lacked the full-blown concert hall fervor I had treated Nora to, but Niraj and Paras seemed to appreciate my toilet humor for a few fleeting seconds.

As we all nursed bottled cola, our attention turned to a small wooden chess board that Niraj was setting up while Paras sorted out the game pieces. "Who do you think will win?" Niraj asked me mischievously, knowing that I was a person of manners, despite my giardia song, who would be conflicted with the possible answers – to their entertainment. Sensing a challenge, I went with the safe answer, not wanting to favor one over the other in case one should fall off a cliff.

"Hmmm, I am for both of you," I retorted, resting my chin on my folded arms on the table. They laughed and focused on the battle before them. Each opponent moved skillfully, each move capturing the full concentration of the other as twilight descended on the village and the clanging of donkey train bells subsided to a light din. After some time, it became clear that my words had proven almost prophetic: neither man could defeat the other. The game was a stalemate. Neither were winners, but neither were losers, to be sure.

"Ha! It is a good thing that you chose to support both of us," Niraj joked. "This is really unbelievable." We packed up the game and retired to the grand room of the lodge. The walls were decorated with European and Nepali mountain sports gear. Usually around this time, late in the evening, a calm descended on our group. To an outsider, it might have appeared as indifference or boredom, but to us it was simply a slow resignation to the seductive invitation of slumber and a calm reflection on the day's small victories and less remarkable oddities.

As we drifted into this public solitude, we lounged on the couches of the dimly-lit room as the Dutch man's wife tended to the warm fire. I sat watching the embers cast a soft glow on Paras' face, who I caught smiling secretly to himself, enjoying the moment.

tukche to ghasa

A fter a night in the relatively luxurious guesthouse, we hit the trail early through a landscape much different than anything we'd encountered yet. The Kali Gandaki narrowed, the rocks turned a shade of battleship grey, and evergreen forests grew denser. Between the Dhaulagiri and Annapurna I, the gorge was technically the deepest in the world, and even older than the Himalayas. As the Indian subcontinent crashed into Asia, the river dug into the rising earth like a knife through butter. The landscape was more reminiscent of alpine Europe, or what I imagined the Washington State wilderness to look like. The air was cool, but not too cold. It was fresh, but not so devoid of moisture that it burned the nostrils like match heads with each breath. The wind howled, but it didn't wick every ounce of moisture out of you as it passed. We were definitely entering a new climate zone, and new challenges. From this point on, the trail became rockier, donkey train traffic increased, and the Kali Gandaki we followed no longer gashed the surface of the earth but carved a deep groove into it. It flowed with water colored like molten pewter. The trail was becoming more treacherous, but unknown to us, it was going to get even worse.

The Kali Gandaki valley's dimensions are awe-inspiring, with 20,000-foot (6,000 meter) peaks in almost every direction. Every morning, the same turboprop airplane that brought us up to Jomsom wound through the valley like a barnstormer buzzing past us, racing to get to Jomsom before the winds picked up. The valley was so massive that the twin-engine aircraft looked like a child's toy. The low altitude pass every day, and the return pass to Pokhara an hour later were exciting to watch, and reminded me of a close air support pass in combat.

"Man, you need to take that thing off," Paras said, half joking. "You look like a terrorist or something. It may confuse people." Speaking of close air support in combat, I was wearing an olive green Arab scarf, called a *keffiyeh* or *shemagh*. I'd had it since Iraq. It's an extremely practical piece of gear, and I rarely go on a trip without it. A warm scarf in winter, a cooling head cover in summer, it can be used to keep dust and harsh sunlight from your face. One practice I adopted from the Army and Middle Easterners was avoiding short pants and short sleeves when trekking. It protected the skin from harmful UV rays, irritating dust, and kept my body temperature low. Ever since I was a child going to the beaches of Charleston, South Carolina, I abhorred sunscreen lotion. Its chemical smell and oily consistency made me feel like I was being lathered with a petroleum-based margarine stick, "I can't believe it's not butter!" or rather, "I can't believe it's not toxic!"

"A terrorist? Really?" I replied.

"Yes!" Paras chuckled. "You should see the looks you are getting in the villages. They can't see your face, and I think that makes them uncomfortable."

He was right. My Lawrence of Arabia costume was effectively keeping the elements out, like sunlight and the constant cloud of dust kicked up in my face, but maybe it was too much. It was wrapped tightly around my face, leaving only space for my eyes, which were covered by sunglasses. I looked more like an overweight Hezbollah ninja and less like travel author Rick Steves – although I am not sure you would want either walking through your neighborhood. I would have to take the *Arabian Nights* look down a notch or two, effective or not, and apply a bit of sunscreen. I rewrapped my *keffiyeh* using a technique two Iraqi translators carefully taught me. Like a father teaches a son how to tie his first tie, they showed me the steps while mortar rounds exploded outside our building in Najaf. Now with more of a business casual Tuareg look, face exposed, I was less likely to look like Osama bin Laden in hiding, and more like an eccentric western tourist.

"Were they really looking at me weird?" I asked.

"Uh, yes. You have to remember, these are not Arab people. This dress is foreign to them, too." Arabs, and in some cases Muslims, apparently didn't have the best reputation in this region. When talking with random people on the trip, and casually asking about the large mosque in Kathmandu, one gentleman replied "they make trouble wherever they go. They are trying to take over the world." In September 2004, the BBC reported that Islamic terrorists in Iraq massacred 12 Nepalese laborers because they "came from their country to fight the Muslims and to serve the Jews and the Christians." Of course this was nonsense, fascist propaganda. These same bloodthirsty groups were killing their own Arab, mostly Muslim "brothers" in huge numbers. The beheading of one Nepali worker and shooting of the others led to heavy rioting in Kathmandu and a government ban on Nepalese working in Iraq. Like the huddled masses of scrawny men I saw in the glistening halls of Doha's airport, Nepalese were working crap jobs, building glass and steel edifices to Arab rulers, and serving lobster to U.S. soldiers on combat bases in Iraq. Crap work, but relatively good pay. But, the Nepali government decided their bargain labor prices needed to include some quality shipping and handling fees befitting of human beings, and not treatment like the donkey trains we encountered.

For what they lacked in riches while abroad, the Nepalese made up for it in dignity. With a reputation for hard work, unwavering commitment and honor, the Nepali diaspora had a reputation as solid as Mount Everest. Whether a modest line cook in a restaurant in Virginia or maid in Australia, the foot soldiers of the Nepali quest for opportunity abroad could be found toiling away faithfully, hoping for a better future for their children. The countless signs for "Oxford Academy" and "Harvard School" dotting the cities, poor children dressed in dignified, pressed white uniforms, all suggested that these were a people who knew the value of hard work, of honor, of the power of education and importance of education...even if it meant working like a slave to get the next generation there.

Some of the most famous Nepalese represented abroad are the Gurkhas. British Field Marshal Sam Manekshaw, Chief of Staff of the Indian Army, once remarked, "If a man says he is not afraid of dying, he is either lying or is a Gurkha." Known for their warrior prowess, the Gurkhas have served in militaries across the world, most famously with the British Army for over 100 years. They have received the Victoria Cross 26 times, and are entrusted with security at U.S. Navy ports in the Middle East and embassy facilities in Afghanistan. Retired British Army Gurkhas can go on to lucrative security contracts and sometimes settle in Great Britain or Hong Kong. But despite their honorable service, they have struggled for equal pension entitlements to their comrades in the British Army, and settlement rights. The Gurkha Welfare Trust has been established out of the UK to help offset the hardships faced by Gurkhas returning home to poverty and limited medical facilities. Unlike the cowards terrorizing innocent people in the Middle East and ruining the reputation of a whole people, the Gurkhas and Nepalese like them have selflessly and often thanklessly labored for a better future, boosting Nepal's reputation around the world. For many familiar with the Nepali work ethic abroad, it's clear that the people are what make Nepal truly special, not simply its landscape.

Navigating the new landscape along our route meant using a number of cable bridges. Some of these seemed to stretch as far as a football field across deep ravines, allowing no margin for error. Looking like something out of *Indiana Jones*, the bridges were wide enough for two people to pass, and floored with aluminum plates instead of rotting wood. Depending on their sturdiness, donkey train drivers let the entire herd cross at once, or just a few at a time. Like a trampoline, the structure bounced with every step we took, increasing with intensity towards the center, which terrified Nora. It didn't help that I teased her about the cables being frayed or the bolts creaking. Sure, if you weren't paying attention, your foot could slip between gaps in the plates, but for the most part, these bridges were solid. In fact, they were pretty amazing feats of engineering, considering the logistical challenges and terrain.

Getting good childcare in these parts also seemed like a challenge. We walked into a small settlement of whitewashed stone huts along a ravine, and Niraj spotted what looked like a little garden gnome at the ledge of a 50-foot (15 meter) drop. He suddenly jogged ahead of us and scooped up the creature. It was a baby no older than a year, dressed in a hooded purple cape and tattered green pants playing a game of pickup sticks mere inches from the ledge. I'm not sure if Himalayan kids are born with some kind of disregard for heights, like mountain goat kids, but as Niraj took the little garden-elf look-a-like by her tiny hand and walked her back to her house, it was clear that he'd just averted disaster. As he searched the neighboring houses for an adult, I wondered what people up here did when they were sick or injured. There were no hospitals, no ambulances, and unless you counted the dreadlocked Sadhus walking by, no doctors. Little did I know, I was about to get a first hand lesson in what happens when your luck runs out in the middle of nowhere.

Sadhus may not be medical doctors in the modern sense, but the authentic ones did command some respect. They wouldn't be able to perform open heart surgery or heal a compound fracture for a baby who'd just fallen off a cliff, but they could bring you blessings, especially if you helped them along their way. That is what Niraj and Paras explained while we talked to a younger Sadhu on the trail. Draped in a marigold-colored tunic and what looked like shards of oriental carpets, the easygoing holy man brushed the trusses of dreadlocks from his face so I could take his photograph – with his permission. After all, these people were individuals with a right to privacy. Nepal was not a zoo, and these houses were not part of an amusement park. How would it feel if Nepali tourists came to America and poked their heads in my doorway and took photos of my children without asking? Pretty weird, of course!

As Paras and Niraj mentioned, there were the real Sadhus and the freeloading Sadhus. This Sadhu received their seal of approval. We chatted with him and found out he was headed to Muktinath, like the other pilgrims we'd been passing in greater numbers. Clearly, there was going to be a huge festival up in the hills we had left days earlier. The holy man's younger complexion betrayed less experience; perhaps a recent recruit to the ascetic life. He explained that he was a successful student in the city, an entrepreneur who had decided to give it all up. *Thar's spiritual gold in them ther hills*, he seemed to say, pointing at the peaks. How long would his journey last? Did he sign a permanent contract with the gods? Not really. He explained that wisdom was the goal, and if and when he reached it, he would likely return to worldly life.

We continued on and entered Kalopani with an American walking alongside us. He spoke to his companion like the anti-Sadhu, desperately seeking the worldly life. Wearing an Australian-style bush hat and mint condition trekking clothes – without a rucksack – he trailed behind his friends. Dressed more like they were part of a corporate teambuilding exercise, with porters carrying their gear way in front of them, they seemed to be more on the block checker circuit.

"Nepal my ass," he muttered under his breath. "I don't see why people come all the way here for this shit."

"Hurry the fuck up! You are slowing us down," his companions teased him.

I really wondered why people like this came out to Nepal at all? Was it the bragging rights? The travel shows made it look easy from the comfort of the couch back in the living room, but traveling in any developing country is hard work. It's mentally demanding, and physically taxing. Your brain is a sponge taking in a totally new landscape, people, smells, tastes, and hazards. It's an extremely rewarding experience, but it also consumes a lot of energy. It also requires a lot of fluids if you are infested with a parasite.

Just as this Napoleon Dynamite-meets-Rick Steves character passed, Nora and I were holding the tiny hands of schoolchildren walking home along our way.

"Do you know how much longer it is to the next town?" he asked abrasively, mouth agape and dragging his hiking poles behind him. He cut an underwhelming figure with this slumped shoulders and fanny pack.

"Dunno, probably about another hour or so," I answered.

"Uh huh," he scoffed, "No one seems to know where they are around here!"

I raised my eyebrow at him and wished he'd move along. He stumbled along further, asking random villagers about the next town.

"Doooo youuuu knowwww next towwwwnnnn? Hooow loooooong?"

The villagers looked at him strangely, wondering who this condescending, panting, suburban stranger was. Better yet, some of the young men played along, acting the fool.

"Mister, I am not sure, let me ask my friend how far is it."

"Ah yez, you goin' to next town? I think that two hour. Yez, and wery dangerous and hard," the friend nodded in exaggerated contemplation. "Maybe you fall?"

"You've got to be kidding me!" he cried, falling for their ruse.

"Yes, and you see ahead, it very bad. You have to walk down cliff. Yes, maybe you fall?"

Now, on that point, they were not joking. The path leading out of the settlement suddenly disappeared into a gaping hole in the earth. We decided to take a break and rest on a knoll for a quick nap in the shadow of Annapurna I. Nora lay in the grass and shut her eyes in perfect bliss, peeking from the corner of her eye at me chuckling as the Napolean Dynamite of trekking attracted a small crowd.

"I have money and I am willing to pay someone to take me to the next town. I have more money than you can imagine. I can't walk anymore, so I'll pay your brother, uncle, or whoever to take me," he pouted.

Whenever you are in a foreign country, or anywhere for that matter, it's not a good idea to let people know you are desperate, have cash on you, and will pretty much accept any offer. This is like going into a Turkish bazaar in Istanbul and telling the carpet dealer you are rich, have a flight to catch in an hour, and need a present for your wife's birthday tomorrow. But something unexpected happened when a man, as promised, showed up on a motorcycle.

With a streetwise swagger, the young driver popped his helmet off and stood next to his bike, looking at the tourist skeptically.

"Where you goin'? You a hippie?"

"No, of course not! I'm going to the next town. So let's go. I want you to take me down the hill."

"You know, this naw free. Petrol esspenssive."

"I've got more money than you can imagine, than you make in a whole year," he overconfidently announced, as if to secure his superiority; to coerce this man.

"Ah, yeah?"

"Yeah. It's a fact. So how much to get to the next town?" Obviously he wasn't so good with money. He let the other set the price first.

"Five dollar."

"What?! Five dollars?! There is no way. Here; here are three dollars."

I thought five bucks was perfectly reasonable for what would be a quantum leap for this sorry excuse for an outdoorsman. But this wasn't about money anymore. This was about teaching an overgrown brat a lesson in humility.

"OK, 20 dollar."

"What?! You must be kidding!"

"No, I make for you – sp'essal offer: 1,000 dollar!" he nodded as his friends grinned.

"OK, OK, I'll pay five dollars! Here, here you go," he shuffled bills out of his wallet.

"Ah, no probrem. 8,000 dollar!" The men standing around shot mischievous glances at each other while holding back laughter. "10 dollar. Let's go!"

The tourist stood indignantly looking around for sympathy, but he wasn't getting any from me. In such a poor country, where fuel is in short supply, the driver's original price was reasonable, but the tourist's behavior wasn't. Sure, the driver could overlook it, but he decided his dignity was more valuable. Not only that, the tourist learned an important lesson: money can't buy you everything. Dignity and respect matter in this country. It's a form of currency – currency he couldn't find in that wallet of his. The man slowly swung his leg over the back seat of the motorbike and it sunk deeply with his weight before they drove off.

The cliff trail was more like a mountain goat trail covered in loose gravel. Hopping from one level to the next, I landed top-heavy each time, thanks to the kitchen sink I'd packed along with me. I was such an idiot to pack so much, and cursed myself repeatedly. At a few points, my boots skidded to the edge of the trail, peaking over the edge of a sheer drop. If this wasn't bad enough, porters in flip flops carrying oversized loads slid past. I couldn't figure out if their shaking bodies were simply steadying their loads or terrified of being swallowed up by the ravine below. One wrong move and one of us would surely be condor food in no time. Going downhill is not always as appealing as it sounds, indeed the western tourists coming uphill looked terrified, too. While my muscles strained to keep balance, theirs were beginning to fail on the ascent.

I wouldn't wish this on my enemies, I thought when we finally made it to level ground. None of us needed to talk about how difficult the trail was. We just looked at each other knowingly. We were in this together. There was no turning back, especially now. There was no way I was going back up that cliff for anything. We were committed to crossing anything that lay between us and the next wheels back to Pokhara. There was plenty to worry about now that the trail was getting hairier. Little did we know that this was just the beginning.

There is something, though, that happens in a mind that knows it has no other choice but forward. Like the soldier deployed to combat, he doesn't try to fight it. He finds ways to cope with it, to make it somehow manageable – numb himself to it while focusing on getting home safe. Combine this with the meditative cadence of the Annapurna Circuit, and you can almost feel like the trail has the same effect as Jesus calling Peter out of the fishing boat to walk on water, except you are sometimes walking a path as wide as an index card with a sheer drop below. But you do it without thinking anymore, because you have to have faith. You have no other choice. No helicopter is coming for you. You aren't going to walk back uphill to Jomsom airstrip several days away. Prayerful momentum becomes the wind at your back.

The old women in bright saris embroidered with gold thread knew this as they passed, headed for Muktinath. Exchanging *namastes* with us, these faithful navigated the same tough terrain in nothing but slippers and shower shoes. I was in awe of them, really. They had an ordinary gym bag slung over the shoulder by the handles while carrying a wooden staff in the other hand – not even breaking a sweat. They didn't need a motorcycle to get them anywhere on their pilgrimage – and they were going *uphill!* Groups of these women traveled together like small sororities. Few men were among them, and I noticed they looked less Mongolian, with slimmer facial features than in the highlands. With their colorful dress and suntanned faces, they bore an uncanny resemblance to Native Americans. When I thought about it more, the shamanistic influences, the music, the dress, and the appearances seemed vaguely Native American. Of course, these were simple tourist musings, but I wondered if the Native Americans originated out of Nepal and the Tibetan region.

There comes a point, usually at about 5 p.m., when everyone unanimously agrees that it's time to end the trek for the day. That time came as we entered the outskirts of Ghasa and its lush green fields of wheat waving in the wind like a giant emerald bed sheet being laid out. The day had been long, and the temperatures had grown hotter as we descended, continuing past an endless procession of colorfully-dressed pilgrims heading to Muktinath. Paras and Niraj had done exceptionally well at finding lodging at local tea houses up to this point, but on this particular day, day five for us on the Annupurna Circuit, Ghasa had limited accommodations. During the entire trek, we passed the main tourist overnight stops for less popular villages. In Ghasa, the colorful "Hotel Florida" looked inviting, but Niraj came outside disappointed after inspecting the rooms. "It's no good," he advised. "We should continue to the edge of town." I was growing tired, all my energy spent after a day in the heat and strong afternoon winds. I hoped we would find relief soon, but as we continued to the edge of town, there were only a few stone barns and some random people idly walking around. There was something different about this village. The people were quieter, more dismissive; perhaps indifferent towards westerners. They looked weary and distrustful. There were no friendly greetings or loud "*namaste!*" calls.

I was beginning to wonder if we'd have to hike another few kilometers to find lodgings. The next settlement was hours away in Talbagar, and that was just a guess. After another 15 minutes of trekking, we came to a small settlement. It was the last one as far as the eye could see. Clouds were growing and a light sprinkle of rain began to fall as Paras and Niraj entered a whitewashed guesthouse to inquire about rooms and space. Regardless of what they found, it was clear that we would stay there for the night. Nora and I waited outside with our rucksacks resting along a wall as pilgrims passed by. An old man on the guesthouse patio sat and strangely observed us. Niraj and Paras returned and signaled that they'd arranged our stay for the night.

As was our custom, Nora and I parted the guys for our respective rooms to relax for about an hour before heading down to the dinner table. By then, Paras and Niraj were usually already sitting and chatting with the innkeepers. Entering a new guest room was always an afternoon. After a long day of walking and aching muscles, I always looked forward to opening the door of our new room to see what surprises awaited us. In the strange town of Ghasa, there was not much to get excited about. The floor consisted of dirty concrete, the walls were sloppily painted, and dozens of arthropods like spiders and centipedes crawled across the bed. If someone brought me to the place blindfolded, I would have thought I was in a Burmese prison cell. But strangely, the bathroom was immaculate, with all of the utilities you would expect from a budget western hotel.

"We should move our beds into the bathroom!" I joked with Nora.

She was a trooper. After a long day of trekking, she didn't rest after we entered our room. She offered her usual amusing commentary on the room's interior, and expressed her dismay or pleasure with the bathroom. As I did each time we entered a new bedroom, I dropped my rucksack on the floor and fell face-first into the bed, being careful not to get anything dirty. Ignoring the scent of wet dog in the sheets, my evening ritual of lying comatose began. Half dreaming, I heard several explosions boom over the valley. It sounded oddly like the countless mortar attacks on my base in Iraq. It turned out to be thunder, but for a moment, I was caught in a kind of mild war flashback brought on by sounds, my Third World surroundings, and exhaustion. It was hard to imagine that during the Maoist insurgency, it was possible villages like this were mortared or echoed with violence.

I lay there totally incapacitated, responding to Nora's evening room assessment with groans of approval or sympathy. With my mouth blissfully parted and face pressed against the mattress, my aching body rested limply in a way to produce the most satisfying sensation of recovery. It was intoxicating to lie there and explain to Nora how I felt as if I had been run over by a truck, while with her endless energy she prepared for the evening dinner by taking a shower. Grudgingly, I pulled myself from my drunken state on the bed and woke up. I then stood under the warm shower for a minute or two, moaning in approval of the water's healing temperature.

We walked down to the kitchen to eat dinner with the guys, who were waiting for us. They were looking rough, with drowsy eyes and obligatory smiles. Their bodies were tired, but they were in good spirits, as always. As we all sat at a long table near the kitchen in the poor guesthouse and exchanged a few laughs about our aching bodies, we noticed a boyish-looking man smiling widely and eagerly at us – as if amazed by our presence. We all glanced at each other at the table and exchanged amused grins. What was he doing?

It turned out that our smiling companion was the waiter. He approached us courteously and took our orders, smiling intensely the whole time. It was like a happy grimace, purely benevolent and hiding no condescension. We thought it was odd, if not humorous. When he continued to gush, I proposed that he may be interested in Paras or Niraj. Paras laughed and shook his head, politely distancing himself from my nonsense. That opened the conversation to other theories about why our host was so happy. We had a great time amusing ourselves and laughing until he brought our orders of Dahl Bhat, pizza, Coca-Cola, mashed potatoes and French fries, almost an hour after we placed our order. Then, he uncomfortably grimaced, cast his eyes down at the floor, and said something in Nepalese. Paras and Niraj grew uncomfortable and nodded to him.

"What did he say?" Nora asked.

"He said that his head is hurting," Niraj replied.

We interpreted that to mean that he was mentally disabled to some degree that we had not noticed. We all sat around the table and looked at each other, feeling terrible about having so much fun at his expense. It was never malicious, but rather the punch-drunk giddiness that captured us each night around the dinner table after a long day of trekking. Feeling like a complete asshole, I stirred my mashed potatoes and secretly begged God for forgiveness. What could my penance for this possibly be?

Two German women entered the dining room at dusk chatting to themselves in German. They had just entered the village after a long trek up from Tatopani, famous for its hot springs, and threw a perfunctory nod our way.

"Do you mind if vee zmoke?" one said with a thick German accent, triggering Mike Meyers' "Sprockets" skits in my head.

I was rather enjoying the fresh air the light rain brought with it. The air was cool, fragrant, and refreshing in this damper climate zone. Why would anyone in their right mind think it was okay to smoke indoors in such a place, to fill the air with toxic exhaust, to force their chemical addiction, their personal weakness, on others? You don't travel to the Himalayas to suck up the cigarette smoke.

"Agh, why do Germans smoke so much?" I asked in German. I couldn't help it. But after hearing how Americans are fat, stupid, carbon-dioxide spewing warmongers more than once from these people, I thought there was something deeply egoistic, if not cynical, about thinking anyone would want to suck up their pollution. It was true. Back in Germany you could find a cigarette machine on almost every corner. After spending an overcast, nuclear winter-like cold season indoors, the sheer joy of sitting in the sun during the short German summer at a street café was often ruined by the constant stench of cigarette smoke. These offenders, while careful to keep the cancer sticks far from their own faces between fixes, would let their poison waft over in the faces of children and pregnant women without thinking twice. The German smoker was a kind of authoritarian dictator in my mind. Forcing others to consume their bad habit, sometimes even their own children, which is a scumbag thing to do. Ironically, some of the most organic food eating, hippy, anti-nuclear friends of mine were chain smokers, claiming it was a small release from stress. While I occasionally smoked at a bar, and only then enough times to count on one hand in a year, it was certainly a form of slavery, mindless obedience. How could someone eat organic food and claim to be a rebel while poisoning their own bodies and doling out cash like a zombie to a corporation that profits from their chemical addiction? Asking if someone minded if you smoked was the equivalent of asking someone you don't know if they mind if you climb up on their table and fart directly into their face for the next 10 minutes because it pleasures you. Yes. I did mind if they smoked.

Like true addicts, the two women looked offended. "I would not consider three cigarettes a lot," a leathery skinned German woman croaked with the tell tale signs of a rusty larynx. I shrugged my shoulders.

We started a conversation in German and they asked where I was from in Germany. "Amerika," I said. It was like dropping a bomb, adding insult to injury. Eyes rolled, brows furrowed, and noses tilted skywards. Rudeness between Germans may be forgivable. It's a kind of working class banter, which is why I didn't mind being direct with them. These were the rules of engagement, after all. But this kind of directness from an American was practicing Germaness without a license. The conversation didn't last long after that.

The two women ordered Everest beers, which our smiling waiter brought promptly and began to open at their table. With a confident flick of his wrist, the bottle top opened and spewed beer all over the place. It had undoubtedly been shaken rigorously during its journey on the donkey train. The women were appalled and demanded a towel, but he opened the second bottle in a similar way with it exploding its contents onto the women and the table. All the while, the waiter smiled, not realizing how angry the women were. We chuckled again as the women relocated to another table and demanded fresh mayonnaise for their salad.

"This mayonnaise is old," exclaimed one of the women. The waiter did not understand their heavy accents (and we were unsure whether he could understand us at all) and returned with more bad mayonnaise. The women grew angrier, but I thought it was a bit pompous to expect German-quality mayo in such a rural village. The two ordered another beer and cautiously instructed the waiter how to open the bottle without the explosive results from earlier. The waiter looked on smiling, but showed some signs of frustration. The women were losing patience with him and had not caught on that he was disabled. We explained to them that he seemed to be disabled. They seemed to think that was his own fault and he shouldn't be a waiter if he was so afflicted.

As Paras and Niraj picked through their Dal Bhat with unusual indifference, the thick smell of human waste began wafting through the air at the dinner table. The toilet was next to the kitchen door. Paras got up and shut the door. But then something disturbing happened. A village girl ran into the kitchen screaming frantically with tears streaking down her dirty face. We were all startled, and Paras and Niraj tried to make sense of what she was saying. The man of the house left urgently with the girl into the darkness. Something seemed to be seriously amiss in the small settlement of only four or five structures. We were in the middle of nowhere, miles away from the nearest settlement resembling a real village. I thought about the stories we had heard about local soldiers getting drunk and shooting people, but watched Niraj's face for a sign of danger. He seemed unbothered. "A father is drunk and holding a knife to his eldest son's neck," he said.

"Have you ever seen the Alfred Hitchcock movie *Psycho*?" I asked. "This place is giving me the creeps," I said, genuinely feeling a bit uncomfortable despite the trekking giddiness.

"Yes, this place is no good," Paras agreed while bobbing his head, "and the Dal Bhat does not taste good." If the Dal Bhat isn't good, then the guesthouse can't be good – call it the *Dal Bhat standard*. Nora and I decided it was time to call it a night and excused ourselves for the evening. Niraj and Paras stayed at the table and chatted with the Germans as we went to our room, and I jammed my aluminum trekking poles between the wooden door and the floor to keep any loony intruders out. As always, we fell asleep quickly and deeply. We would need the rest for what lay ahead.

10

ghasa to tatopani

We got up early so that we could depart Ghasa without delay. As we stood around filling our Camelbaks with bottled water, the handicapped waiter dashed out to the porch to see us off. Grinning ear to ear, he waved to us like we were celebrities and shouted some encouraging words. Sure, he was handicapped, but his simple joy and enthusiasm was contagious. I smiled to myself, having learnt a basic lesson over again that I should have never forgotten: don't judge a book by its cover. We waved back to him, and he could hardly control himself, jumping up and down as we took our first steps of the morning. You'd think we were best friends, and maybe he felt like that in his mind, but it had the effect of making me feel that we were too. Feeling terrible for making fun of him, I turned around and waved goodbye one more time to the Nepali fellow who taught me a beautiful lesson.

If I needed to clear my conscience through penance, an opportunity at redemption was right around the corner. The trail quickly became treacherous, crawling in a ribbon of loose gravel alongside the sheer vertical drops into the Kali Gandaki below. By now, the river cut a ravine so deep it could only be heard, not seen. We heard more donkey trail bells than ever before and increasingly had to share the narrow trails with the sad beasts.

Donkey trains were the lifeline of this part of the Annapurna Circuit. Usually in cohorts of about ten animals, these four-legged pickup trucks moped along the trail carrying everything from crates of beer to propane tanks on their sides. With bulky cargo strapped to their bloated bellies, they dominated smaller trails and forced anything in their way to flatten themselves along the rock walls, or risk being pushed over a cliff. Young men acted as train drivers, mercilessly tossing rocks onto the backs of the beasts to keep them moving along. Some trains were better cared for than others. Some animals were groomed, decorated with colorful ribbons, and loaded reasonably. Others were mangy, scabbed with sores and cigarette burns, their hooves struggling to find solid ground beneath. Sometimes they didn't. As we crossed the longest suspension bridge yet, I looked down into an abyss. Any false move on this section of trail would be fatal.

Today proved to be fatal for one road worker. Hiking along the edge of the ravine, we noticed small dots, like ants, along the opposite side. A closer look revealed they were men walking along nightmarishly steep rock faces like mountain goats. The men were building a road north along the route in what we were told would make the Annapurna Circuit passable with vehicles, not just foot traffic and donkey trains. Without any level ground to pave, these men were literally chiseling a route directly into the side of the ravine with their bare hands. I watched in disbelief as a man squatted, holding out a chisel while another scrawny man raised a sledgehammer and came crashing down right at the chisel head. They did all of this in a space that looked to be about as wide as a sidewalk, without hardhats, jackhammers, gloves — or even a rope to keep them from falling more than 500 feet (150 m) below into the Kali Gandaki whitewater. I later wrote a research paper about road construction in Nepal and was shocked to learn that many road workers experienced similar conditions that often proved fatal. Did the guy with the sledgehammer smell like alcohol? Was he going to hit the chisel every time? Would he lose his balance and simply be gulped up by the dark ravine below? Paras and Niraj learned from oncoming traders that a worker fell into the ravine and some villagers were waiting for the body to float downstream. Whether or not it ever did, I don't know, but seeing those men on the cliff hammering away at a mountain with their bare hands for, at the most, a few bucks a week, reminded me of not only how badly Nepal needed sustainable modernization, but also how brave those men were.

Heat could also be fatal. The new climate zone was humid, unlike any other we encountered so far. This combined with the Stairmaster-like workout along the craggy trails meant we were sucking water down at about a liter and a half an hour. Water management became extremely important. In oppressively hot weather, nothing can satisfy like icy, fresh water. It cleans, refreshes, and rejuvenates the body in a way that makes all other beverages seem like sugary syrup. In the highlands of the Annapurna Natural Reserve, an NGO worked with locals to create fresh water stations for foreign trekkers, for a small fee. The system used ozone to kill bacteria and was operated by local villagers. The great thing about the project is that trekkers don't have to pack loads of fresh bottled water and reduce their endurance. There is less plastic bottle waste, because they may be refilled at the stations, and locals benefit from the revenue. The bad thing was that fewer water stations existed at lower elevations for some reason. At the rate we were drinking, we were buying up new bottles whenever we could find them. Water was a lifeline, and we could never drink enough. When we walked into the small village of Dana, we immediately filled our empty Camelbaks for what I thought would be enough for the trip to Tatopani, only a few more kilometers away. Nora, Paras, and Niraj sat along the town street snacking and playing peekaboo with a wide-eyed toddler in a doorway escorted by a healthy looking rooster at his side. Chickens seemed more like house pets than dinner. We nibbled on Snickers bars and took huge gulps of water while nodding to obnoxious trekkers bouncing past without any gear. The Americans would give a "Wuz up" nod, while the Israelis largely ignored any greetings, expressionless through their shades. Like many on this trail, they were just passing through, not looking to socialize with anyone, including Nepali villagers. But maybe that wasn't a bad idea. I looked over to see Niraj cornered by an older gentleman lecturing him about something I didn't understand. He seemed pretty passionate, waving his hands in the air and raising his voice. I wondered if we needed to help extract Niraj, but it turned out the gentlemen was just drunk and looking for a friend. Niraj kindly obliged before giving us a look that said "Let's get out of here!"

We headed out of Dana along a gentle trail with a menacing drop to one side. Some trekkers and their guide had continued on ahead of us and we were glad to let them pass so we wouldn't hear their loud antics echoing in the valley behind us. About fifteen minutes later, just as we were getting back into our cadence, we happened upon a confusing situation. Niraj and Paras looked back at me as I noticed a white woman laying in the brush – motionless. I thought she was dead. Next to her stood an older Nepali man, looking helpless and confused. He was obviously very poor, spoke no English, and did not know what to do. The woman had hired him to be her guide and carry her bags from the village of Tatopani, the popular tourist spot with its rustic restaurants and small hot springs. The American group, which was only a few minutes ahead of us, must have passed by the scene and left her there in a hurry to get to Tatopani. In any case, we suddenly found ourselves in an emergency situation in the middle of nowhere.

I didn't have time to think much. Army training, and especially combat, has a way of making you act first and think later, albeit in a very effective way. Constant practice, all those nights standing in formation for no reason except to learn to follow orders, those 14 months in Iraq – all came together in that moment without thinking twice. I followed the steps I had practiced so many times over the years: assess the situation, send for help, and administer aid. We all cast off our rucksacks and dug out the medical kit I brought from Germany. For the first time on the trail, I didn't feel over-prepared.

I approached the young woman and realized she was in an advanced state of dehydration. She spoke agonizingly, her skin was pale, but most disturbing were her fingers and limbs. They were all curled tightly in the fetal position. She was as stiff as a board, her muscles unable to bend even a few degrees.

"Can you hear me?" I asked.

"It hurts so bad," she croaked in a murmur that hinted at surrender. Her eyes began to flutter and roll back into her head. This was bad. If she lost consciousness, it would be nearly impossible to hydrate her without an IV, which I am trained to administer, but did not have with me. If we lost her now, there was a possibility that she would die. By the looks of her, she wasn't far from death.

"I need you to hear my voice and stay with me," I told her. "I need you to stay awake because we are going to help you get better, okay?" I knew I needed to get into her head, to let her know that she was in good hands and that we knew what we were doing. Without being able to make eye contact, and with her body totally in shock, voice was the only means I had to pull her back from apathy, from giving in to what must have been an irresistible desire to sleep, to let go. Using a commanding but understanding voice would be important, I thought. Letting her pass out wasn't an option as far as I was concerned.

"It hurts," she repeated, her voice fading away. She tried to speak, but only her lips moved. As if she knew this herself, by out-of-body experience or something; she grimaced, knowing that she was not only losing her ability to move, but to speak. Nora and I checked her eyes, which stayed in the back of her head, dilated widely.

"We need to move her away from the cliff and into the shade," I said as I removed my *keffiyeh* and handed it to Nora, Niraj, and Paras. We picked her up and put her in what little shade some brush offered and loosened her clothing. She shrieked terribly as we lifted her, giving me goose bumps and an even greater sense of urgency. Nora and Paras held the *keffiyeh* over her as a canopy protecting her from the intense sun.

"I need you to open your eyes and listen to my voice," I said. "You are going to be okay, but you have to stay awake and listen to my voice." She nodded her head, opened her vacant eyes, and began to cry without any tears. I instructed Nora to grab our baby wipes and place the moist towels on her exposed skin. The wind coming through the valley would help cool the wipes and dissipate some of her body heat. I grabbed a T-shirt from my pack, dampened it with water, and placed it around her neck and head, then began lightly dampening her lips with small droplets of water from my Camelbak water hose, hoping to gradually hydrate her extremities to a point where she could swallow small amounts.

"It hurts, it hurts," she moaned pitifully.

The light breeze in the valley, the moist towels on her skin, canopy cover, and moist T-shirt were beginning to help. I dribbled some water on her clothes and smeared some on her face. In the back of my mind, I knew that we were working with a limited supply of water, and we had to be sure to conserve some emergency reserve, lest we become a casualty ourselves. With my own parasitic infection, it was hard enough to stay effectively hydrated, and even as I gave up my water for her, the dryness in my own mouth was reminder enough that we had to conserve water.

Doing everything we could to get her external temperature down, I focused on coaching her so that she'd overcome any feelings of apathy or surrender. She would need to hydrate if she was going to make it.

"You are doing better," I said, making sure to keep a conversation going with her to lessen the chances of her losing consciousness. That was still a primary concern. "I need you to open your mouth," I instructed her. She painfully complied. I lowered the water hose from my Camelbak and squeezed the nozzle of the mouthpiece, letting a small stream of water into her mouth, then let a small amount flow over her face and lips. We continued with this pattern slowly over fifteen minutes. She began to regain her strength after about thirty minutes, but only slightly.

"You are doing great; you are going to be okay. How do you feel?"

"I...I...am...feeling better," she said in an Australian or British accent. "It feels good." Her beleaguered voice had some tone of hope, of consciousness.

As I continued to alternate between wetting her face and getting her to take small sips of water, Niraj and Paras spoke with the old guide so we could get her information. A crowd of villagers congregated around us looking curiously at the feeble woman and the medical supplies scattered around her. A man with a donkey showed up.

"You need helicopter?" he asked. It didn't sound like a bad idea, but the woman would incur a very expensive bill. In any case, it looked as if she was slowly coming around and there didn't seem to be a suitable landing area for miles. Just in case, I pulled out my GPS and got our coordinates. Niraj and Paras learned that the old man with her was actually her guide, and not a professional one.

"He says that she has been very sick with diarrhea, but decided to leave Tatopani against his advice this morning," Niraj translated. "He doesn't know her name. He has no emergency contact for her and didn't know what to do once she collapsed. She hasn't been drinking bottled water. Just boiled water."

As the woman lay limp in the grass and her limbs slowly came to life from their earlier wooden state, I noticed how poorly prepared she was for her journey – especially the treacherous uphill that awaited her just south of Ghasa. She wore a short sleeve tie-dye cotton shirt with a Nepal motif purchased from a tourist shop, Converse Chuck's tennis shoes, and kaki shorts – not the ideal clothing to protect her body from the elements. Clearly, she was a naïve westerner who thought she was just going for a stroll in paradise in the footsteps of the hippies before her. Obviously, here was someone who failed to obey two key rules of backpacking: respect nature and your body. The Himalayas are not something to be simply conquered and ticked off of a list of things to do during a two-week vacation. They require respect, compromise, and flexibility. These are all great things to realize in the mountains, things that make the Himalayan experience so special and humbling. The "I want it and want it now" approach of the West has absolutely no meaning in those hills.

"I have to shiiiiiit," the woman said quietly but urgently while crying. Nora looked up at me with a puzzled look. I shrugged. We'd have to help her shit, so we reached under her arms and held her up while the villagers looked on. We unfastened her shorts, moved her underwear and I looked away while she sickly defecated in front of us all. She cried all the while, but in far better condition than she was when we found her. We set her aside and continued to hydrate her even though my water was almost empty. Color was returning to her face and she began to hold her head up on her own and make coherent eye contact.

"You are going to be okay," I said again. "You are back with us."

The man with the donkey offered to take her back to Tatopani, but the trail was too rough and it would be difficult to secure her to the animal. Not only that, but I wasn't comfortable letting a semiconscious female traveler be carried off on the back of a donkey by a man I didn't know — and that would be true in any country. By now, a crowd of villagers was trying to get a look at the woman, which was a bad idea since we were cluttered right up against a cliff.

"They are going to have to give us some space or this is going to stress her out," I said to Paras and Niraj, who began backing the crowd away.

During the hour-long ordeal, a few trekkers walked right past us without offering any help or water. I had heard about this type of behavior on Mount Everest, where an "every man for himself" attitude prevails. Some of this is pure arrogance, some of it is a survival instinct to preserve resources, and some of it is a matter of keeping on schedule. So many western trekkers are on a tight, well-planned schedule, goal-oriented, and not interested in any drama that may force them to stop and put their iPod on pause. But, an older, petite French woman trekking uphill stopped for a moment to ask if she could help. I showed her the technique I used to hydrate the woman and she insisted on using her own water, which she planned on refilling in Dana.

Our group continued to pep-talk the woman and prepare her

for a move to a local village uphill. By this time, some of the village men had arrived with a blanket to carry the woman in.

"She is looking much better," the French woman said. "I will take her to the next village so that you can continue on before it gets dark. The trail is rough ahead."

"Are you sure? Let me give you some hydration salts and diarrhea pills to give her once you get to the village."

"Yes, that would be good. I will stay with her in the village until she is fit again," she promised.

We asked the woman if she was okay with continuing to the village with the French woman, who appeared to have some professional medical training. She approved. Then, once we all agreed on the plan, a Nepali man from the village prepared a harness like an adult-sized baby carrier on his back and we brought the woman to him. He hoisted her upon his back and she held on under her own strength.

"Thank you very much," I said to the French woman. "Here are the medications and a business card for her with my information on it."

"Yes, do not worry. I will make sure she is okay and that we call for a doctor. She is very lucky that your group found her."

"Yes, so many people passed her. Thanks for your help!"

We gathered our things and stuffed our rucksacks with the medical kit and other items that had fallen out during the ordeal so that we could continue on towards Tatopani before it was too late. The landscape became more jungle-like and even more humid. The trail was becoming more primitive – a hardly discernable goat trail of loose stone sometimes less than a foot wide in the side of a valley, with the Gandaki River roaring loudly far below. My mouth was dry and gummy with dehydration, I had a slight headache, and I pinched my water pouch to find only a few drops of warm water left.

"Damn it, I'm going to need something to drink, from someone else." I knew water was non-negotiable on the trail, especially when I was drinking for two: me and a thirsty parasite. I didn't want to be a drag on the group, but they all pitched in some as we wound our way along the cliff sides of a totally new, Amazonian-like valley shrouded in fog. We walked silently together with a sense of urgency. We knew we needed to get to Tatopani without delay. All of us were thinking about how close we'd come to seeing someone die. I know we were also thinking about the people who not only left her on the trail to suffer on her own, but those people who passed us while we were reviving her without even offering to help. It was a disappointing chapter on the trip, but also redeeming in that we were able to help.

"You saved that girl's life, man," Niraj looked me in the eye and said as we walked. "She was gone. How did you know what to do?"

"My Army training took over."

"That's good that you remember."

Clouds began to form and a light rain fell, which was a total blessing. My water was empty, my heart was pumping, but the cooler air and small rain droplets kept me barely fit enough to trek. Each droplet was precious on my skin.

Entering the outskirts of Tatopani, the damp air, cloudy sky, and overgrown stone buildings looked like something straight out of an *Indiana Jones* film. The area was far more wet and humid than the higher elevations – and muddier. We came upon the main street in the small town and noticed the usual assortment of tourist shops with hand-painted signs. Rainwater flowed along the dirty street's gutter that acted as a sewer and wash basin. Women cleaned clothes in the gutter with stones and soap as restaurant runoff flowed in nearby and dogs and chickens sipped the cocktail a little downstream. The lower we went in elevation, the dirtier the towns seemed to be. The locals seemed subdued, loitering in idle groups of men and women, indifferent to the colorfully dressed western backpackers trotting by.

I smelled marijuana wafting through the air and looked over at a restaurant porch to see the American group that passed the dying woman getting stoned and drinking beer. They must have just checked in their stuff at a hotel and were unwinding for the day, laughing and joking all the while.

"Hey, did you guys see that girl fallen next to the trail a while back?" I asked them.

"Yeah, why?" one replied, both of his companions no longer laughing.

"She almost died and people were walking by her leaving her there for dead."

"Oh, well, we didn't know she was that bad."

"Well that is a really shitty thing to do – leaving someone to die – but I hope you guys have a great time anyways and go home feeling proud of yourselves."

"Dude, we're sorry," they replied as I walked off.

Niraj and Paras found a good hotel for all of us and we checked in. Nora and I went up to our room and unloaded our things. I felt light as air getting rid of my pack every afternoon, and fell face first into bed to relax my muscles. A light rain tapped gently on the corrugated steel roof, and all was foggy outside of the windows. I felt like I was in the Great Smokey Mountains of North Carolina, except an incredible view of a snow-covered Himalayan peak could be seen right through our bedroom window as if it was a framed picture.

Before heading downstairs from our lodge room, I watched the churn of people from my window. A bored, young soldier dressed in blue fatigues paced idly and occasionally checked tourist papers with mild interest. A scruffy old man, clearly intoxicated, ostracized himself under a skimpy sheet of corrugated steel as a light rain pattered on his makeshift shelter. He shouted incoherently at a throng of older women sitting opposite him in a shed emblazoned with hand-painted signs offering boot and sewing repair within minutes. They stared emotionlessly at the drunk old fellow as he growled and shouted for his audience. Somehow I got the feeling that this was routine street entertainment for the locals. I slowly drew the curtain before my face and grinned, turning to Nora and strapping my sandals on. It was time to join Paras and Niraj for dinner at the small restaurant below.

Niraj and Paras were already at the Spartan restaurant when we arrived. They had already taken a quick nap while Nora and I recovered in our rooms. After such a harrowing hike, I decided to splurge and order some grilled chicken and a Coca-Cola. Despite my stomach drama and lack of appetite earlier, I needed something hardy, something grilled, something other than the watery potato porridge I ate the night before.

Thirty minutes after ordering my feast, a friendly waiter brought our long-awaited meal to the table. I could hardly contain my laughter looking down at the charcoal black piece of flesh resembling a large human thumb that sat singularly before me as if just pulled from a burning car. My dreams of poultry pleasure suddenly came back down to earth. But, not giving up, I took an earnest chomp on the tiny, soot-encrusted morsel; sorting out layers of grainy crust with my tongue to find a tender strand of good meat. I was almost ashamed of myself.

Along the entire journey up to this point, scrappy chickens could be found pecking away at nothingness, and yet somehow living to see another day. In rubbish heaps, drainage pools, and dirt paths, chickens nourished themselves. In these hills, chicken must be a delicacy. There were few goats or sheep, even fewer water buffalo, and I suspected that the main nourishment came from potatoes and rice. But here, in Tatopani, I decided to splurge on the highest priced menu item – the venerable Himalayan chicken – and was rewarded for my excess accordingly. It should have come as no surprise that my grilled chicken was pitifully malnourished. I was sure that any similar piece of meat would be a treat for a local villager, and regretted bothering the restaurant owner with my TGI Friday's fantasies. Accepting my decision, I scavenged an almond-sized sliver of good meat from the tiny crisp and made a few jokes about it.

"Did you see those women washing their clothes in the gutter?" I asked no one in particular.

"Yes, washing with stones," replied Niraj.

"If only they had washing machines, or some kind of community coin laundry center, that would be cool," I observed, somewhat naïvely, but nonetheless curious.

"Hmmm, I think you would need a lot of electricity for that,"

Paras remarked. "I don't think they have that much up here – at least not enough for that."

During our trek, I noticed how much time is spent doing simple tasks like fetching water and washing clothes – tasks the women spend most of their day shuffling around doing. Laundry in the West was a simple matter of loading and unloading the washing machine and then hanging it up to dry or throwing them in the dryer. In these remote villages, laundry required hours of washing, kneading, stone scraping, twisting, and hanging. Just finding the water to do the task was a challenge, which may explain why the women of Tatopani opted to use the rain-filled gutter. I wondered what they would do with the newfound leisure time should they ever receive washing machines. Would the women have time for other things? What would they do with their newfound time? I knew what I wanted to do with my time in Tatopani.

During our descent from Ghasa, I daydreamed about the paradise of Tatopani with its majestic hot springs. But as we walked from our lodgings down a steep stone stairway to the Kali Gandaki riverbed, my eyes drifted searchingly for an exotic pool of steaming water. Tatopani was something much different though. A simple concrete basin, like a pool for livestock, sat singularly near the edge of the river. It was about 30 feet square and full of ginger-ale tinted water. It wasn't exactly the paradise I had imagined, but the surrounding landscape certainly was. After hiking for so long, I would sit in a dumpster of warm water if I had to.

Despite its modest appearance, the Tatopani springs were a place to relax muscles, nurse wounded feet, and boast about the highlights of adventure on the Annapurna Circuit. As I sat in the warm water relaxing my body, my attention focused on a boisterous British fellow with a large, hairy belly, cunning mustache, and very posh accent. He was the epitome of the cliché British adventurer. As he pressed his prominent belly forward with pride and stretched out his arms in a grand fashion along the spring's wall, he spoke loudly about his trials passing through the Thorong-La – the world's highest trekking pass. Of course, seeing him as unfit as he was, I pondered just how he could have succeeded passing through over 17,749 feet (5,410 meters).

The answer to that question was slowly, almost ashamedly, easing his way toward Nora and me. With downcast and tired eyes, a boy, probably about 15 years old, slipped off his tattered shoes and eased his feet into the water. I recognized him from our trekking earlier in the day. He was a porter, a foot soldier of the Annapurna, carrying bulging gym bags and rucksacks in an almost impossible arrangement slung from a single strap around his forehead. He managed to carry loads surely in excess of 80 pounds upon his skinny frame up and down mountain paths. He managed to hold the strap around his head bearing the incredible weight while pressing on, stumbling lightly on the rocky trails, but with a certain dignity – a certain determination. His presence did not create pity, but rather respect. He wasn't one of the more cosmopolitan porters with proper gear and sharp, profanity-laced English. He was from the country and sweating profusely to make a living charging a lower price than the professional guys. He was the only reason the proud British adventurer conquered Thorong-La.

The porter looked a bit self-conscious, so I welcomed him with a smile and he returned the gesture, seeming more comfortable already. I then realized why he may have been embarrassed. As he drew his mocha brown feet from the steaming water, he methodically massaged what appeared to be the feet of an old man – blistered and splotched with bruises. In particular, his large toenail had split cleanly in the middle and sat concaved on itself. My eyes grew larger as I imagined the pain he must be experiencing. I realized he noticed me looking. He gave a slight shrug and smile as if to say, "Don't worry about it, this is what I do." All the while, the British adventurer spoke in the background about wind that seemed to burn the skin like boiling water high in the pass. He spoke about the Israeli girl who had to be evacuated from the pass by fellow trekkers for attempting to pass in sandals – suffering frostbite. His porter accomplished the transit in a pair of torn, white, Chinese tennis shoes with no grip while carrying a load most people couldn't fit in the trunk of their cars back home. As I imagined him telling the story of his success later in a pub in England, I wondered if he would ever recognize that his success would not have been possible without the 15-year-old boy sitting next to me.

My feet were not doing so well either. Nora and I opted to carry our own, and it showed. As I inspected my tired feet beneath the water, I could see white cushions glowing like ghosts on a pink mass. Some blisters were beginning to form. Worn out Band-Aids slowly detached themselves from my skin in the hot water, leaving a residue like used chewing gum. As I collected my expired Band-Aids with some repulsion, I glanced at the young porter's shoes. How could he walk for miles on end without socks, without insoles, without a proper sole, one with a grip? His shoes, when seen from behind, canted inwards worn away by the trail. He was essentially carrying massive loads while walking with his feet canted inwards. I felt compelled to buy him a new pair of shoes, but there were no shops that I knew of that sold them. Surely, the British fellow noticed that his bargain-priced porter needed some new shoes. I'm just not so sure he cared.

After a relaxing time in the warm Tatopani waters, we withdrew to our lodge rooms and left the awkward group of tourists in the pool – and there really was something awkward about it. I sensed that so many westerners come to Nepal to escape life – to get away from all things and people familiar. Surely, I was there to escape my routine as well. But when you get a group of escapists together, they tend to resent each other's company, because they personify the very society they are trying to detach themselves from. So, groups of tourists grudgingly sit with each other because there is only one Tatopani hot spring – barely exchanging a word. Add to this that many of the tourists are wealthy, there is little room for so many oversized, judgmental egos in one space. That night, I lay in bed thinking of the young man's broken feet. It was at once a testament to the strength of human beings to overcome amazing challenges and a metaphor in some ways of the world order. Whatever it was, I developed a profound respect for the porters of Nepal.

11

tatopani to pokhara

T Under a diamond studded purple night sky, I herded yaks along a silver river somewhere in the Mustang. At least that was what I was dreaming before waking up to pack our bags at five in the morning to leave Tatopani. Groggily stuffing used socks and underwear into my pack, I wasn't ready to leave the Annapurna Circuit. My body begged for the comforts of civilization, but my soul and heart had set delicate roots in the surroundings, like a seedling. I had grown fond of the people, the simple life, and the absence of e-mail and the internet.

I had reached my own kind of *zen*, recalling the Tibetan highlands and pilgrims along the trail. Soon I would be back in Germany, back at a desk, glued to a computer writing stories that literally begged readers to go out and live their lives to the fullest while living in Europe. I wasn't even sure they were listening. Was I even listening to my own heart? Perhaps I was. After asking where I should be in life, I suddenly realized the answer was all around me. I should be in the Himalayas. I should be open to dreams and making them into reality – now. If I had come to Nepal in search of answers, I suddenly realized that I had found them. To paraphrase Mark Twain, it wasn't the things in life you did you may regret, but the things you didn't do.

We weren't waiting for retirement to travel the world. We weren't going to thumb through travel magazines and make hollow promises to friends and ourselves about exploring the world. The world and its opportunities were out there to be had, and it was up to us to open doors, not wait on fate or time to open them up for us.

These thoughts burned in my chest as we opened the door of our lodge and hit the trail with Niraj and Paras. With the Nilgiri mountain towering at our backs, catching the early morning rays, we crossed the rushing Kali Gandaki by way of a thatched vine and root bridge that looked like it would collapse at any moment into the whitewater. We approached another settlement and noticed two boys surrounding a dark object engulfed in smoke. As we came closer, it was clear that this was a goat barbeque. Over a fire of discarded plastic bottles and newspaper, the turgid corpse looked like a terrestrial puffer fish covered in singed, crusty hair. No special barbeque tools are needed when rigor mortis turns the hind legs into perfect rotisserie handles. The amateur cooks laughed at our puzzled looks, shifting the roast's weight side to side by a hind leg, collecting molten plastic and newspaper ash on their dinner. I wondered how they could cook the creature on such a small flame *whole*, without any field dressing at all? Without removing the guts? Surely, the digestive track and other undesirable accompaniments within were boiling and seasoning the insides with *essence de merde*. Niraj and Paras shook their heads grinning, telling us that was definitely not a typical example of Nepali cooking technique.

Down the trail, we encountered another strange site. By the looks of him, this goat wasn't bound for the trash fire. He had a proper collar and some decorations and a proud owner that wasn't manhandling him by the hind legs over toxic smoke. We stopped to take in the rare sight. This goat had a unique deformity: five horns curling like long fingernails from his head. His master paraded him over to us for a closer look and beamed while we took photos of the mutant creature. He claimed it was one of the only examples in the world. I searched the internet later and figured he may not have been off the mark.

The trail became treacherous again, and the river disappeared into a craggy mess of rocks, roaring below us out of sight. The path went from a gently rolling stroll until it gradually rotated 90 degrees along the rocky sides of the gorge. In effect, it disappeared. Donkeys and porters clung to the side of the gorge knowing that one false move would deliver them into the Kali Gandaki with a broken back. We barely made out some commotion in the ravine. A gaggle of overloaded donkeys, legs trembling and reluctant, dotted the same trail we needed to navigate. Sharing the trail with them would be deadly, so we waited for the train drivers to pass. Apparently, someone in the train cautioned us to be careful. They said one of their donkeys just tumbled into the ravine. We looked at each other and mentally prepared ourselves for what looked like the most dangerous leg of the trip so far. We had no other choice than to push on.

The path was a mess. Men carrying impossibly large loads risked their lives. We followed a porter with a cage full of chickens on his back, hoping he would know the way. Taking life-threatening risks, the porter intentionally surfed down rock faces in a controlled crash to shorten the distance needed to creep along. For Nora and me, this was too much. There was no margin for error. Our minds were clear, unlike a few days ago when we experienced a hiker's high and squeezed past road workers on a path not much wider than a tightrope above a sheer drop. Suddenly, our threshold for risk was met. If anything went wrong here in the muddy, rocky ravine, there would be no helicopter ride to safety. Donkey evacuation wouldn't be a good idea, either. We opted to carefully navigate the rougher parts of the trail, even if it meant longer spider-crawling along the ravine walls. Paras and Niraj patiently accommodated our concerns.

All of us hesitated when we finished what we thought was the toughest part of the ravine, only to find a primitive path carved into the side of the wall. It was like a tunnel chiseled haphazardly with one side open in a sheer drop to the whitewater below. The grade was steep, the path was covered in loose stones, there was no guardrail, and whitewater mist created a dangerous Teflon-like surface.

"Man, what the fuck? Are you serious about this?" I asked no one in particular. My heart was pounding like a rabbit being hunted by a pack of beagles.

"Let's go. We have no choice," Paras said with a smile. He coolly moved ahead down the descending path. Niraj took up a position at the rear to coach us along. With her matter-of-fact determination, Nora eased ahead and carefully stepped while shaking her head in disbelief. I stepped forward and cursed all the unnecessary stuff in my rucksack: a pair of socks for every day on the trail, fresh underwear and then some, a change of clothes for every climate. Next time I would be doing laundry on the trail instead of schlepping an entire clothing department with me. *I should have known better*, I thought. I felt like I was walking down an ice-covered sidewalk, downhill, holding a suitcase over my head – like someone walking down a flight of stairs in roller skates with their hands held over their head and no banister to hold on to. This seemed almost suicidal, I thought, looking at the river roaring far below me. I raised my hands over my head and pressed them on the ceiling of the niche. I figured that walking with my feet and hands pressed into the rock above would be more stable, but sure enough, pebbles skidded below my boots like ball bearings.

I slid forward a millimeter, but it felt like a mile. A little further and I would be bounding off the ravine walls like a rag doll before disappearing into the Kali Gandaki for good. Behind me, Niraj asked me to put my hands down and spread them out to keep balance. The path was too loose to take any chances improvising new techniques for traversing it. There is a difference between being scared and being aware of danger. I was aware of the danger and even more so when a donkey train jingled around the bend carefully charging our way. They weren't going to stop for anyone, and I couldn't blame them. After all, who wanted to get a rock to the skull for slowing down? In space as wide as a door frame, we spread ourselves out spread-eagle along the interior wall of the niche, and the donkey trains brushed and bumped past us. Any trekker unwise enough to have taken the exterior side of the path would have been nudged into the ravine as the donkeys droned past, laden with their wide loads of kerosene tanks. It was a climactic end to the final stage of our hike.

Successfully traversing the deadly trail on the sixth day of trekking in the Annapurna, we arrived at our final hiking destination, the small settlement of Rahughat. From there, we had to arrange motor transportation to the smaller town of Beni. We could presumably catch a Tata bus for Pokhara. The settlement had a few small brick lodges, all of them with their blue doors open and chickens pecking around. On the balcony of one lodge were some foreigners with their porters drinking beer in a fraternal celebration marking the conclusion of their trek. Our group was cheerful, but now my thoughts at that point of the trek wandered again. I was having such a wonderful time that I did not want it to end. I could feel those seedling roots of the soul and heart slowly being pulled from the rich soil of the Annapurna. From here on out, we would gradually acclimatize to civilization, first with a truck through the wilderness, then with a bus to the towns, and finally with a tour bus to the bustling metropolis of Kathmandu.

However, it looked like something may have just begun as we offloaded our rucksacks and stretched our legs at a porch where a young lady beckoned us to relax. The shalwar kameez-clad hostess must have been about 25-years-old and seemed to take a liking to Niraj, who was ordering us some drinks and snacks with an air of stoicism. The lady's eyes darted from Niraj to the ground and back while she blushed, and the edge of her lips hinted a smile. With his orders, she took a few self-conscious steps back, and then darted in the kitchen with her scarf whirling behind. I raised my eyebrow and grinned at Paras.

"Hey, it looks like the village girl likes Niraj here...what do you think?" Paras teased.

"Uh, yeah, without a doubt! Did you see her blushing?" I replied. "You may have to come back here, Niraj."

"What are you guys talking about?" he said with a grin. "She is just taking our order. It is nothing. I don't even know what you are talking about."

Paras and Nora chuckled as the lady reemerged with a radiant face betraying embarrassment. If this wasn't love at first sight, then I didn't know what was. She blushed incredibly as she stooped down to Niraj first and served his drink, catching quick glances of him and then looking away hurriedly. Niraj realized we all thought the girl was enthralled with him and appeared somewhat self-conscious. With what looked like a quick curtsey to Niraj, she went on to serve the rest of us before blending into the doorway and watching us for a moment before disappearing again.

"She is definitely in love, Niraj," Paras continued. "Did you see the way that she was looking at you?" We all chuckled again, a bit giddy from our long walk.

"It is nothing at all. She is just being nice to me, nothing more." he replied. Suddenly, the girl returned with some sliced tomatoes and salt for him. Her generosity was beginning to vindicate our suspicions as she gazed adoringly at Niraj, taking great care to place the salt at his disposal before stepping back with a look of anticipation for some sign of approval. Knowing that we were all giggling hilariously inside, Niraj must have felt slightly embarrassed. However, he was a true gentleman and chatted with her a short while, indulging her just enough. Paras looked on with a knowing grin.

"Wow, she seems like a really nice girl," I teased. "Are you going to get her contact information?"

"She is a country girl, and they are nice and generous, generally," he said, dismissing the suggestion that love was in the air. "Alright, let's go!" Niraj said a few minutes later with a smile.

"She loves him so much she brought him an extra treat of tomatoes," Paras joked. "Are you going to come back to see her?" he asked.

I was wondering if that would work at all with Paras and Niraj being Newari, a proud and culturally rich ethnic bloc within Nepal. Their sharper facial features looked less Mongolian than other Nepali people I had seen. Nepal itself is a patchwork of dozens of ethnic groups coexisting within its borders.

"Looks like love to me, Niraj," I joked. "I think you could always come back here and the *tomato girl* would welcome you with open arms! You could come out here and marry and start a trekking lodge with her." We all laughed.

"*Tomato girl* will be waiting a long time," he replied. "I'm not looking for that right now. No time for these things."

We meandered a short distance along a gravel path to a small house that sold tickets for Land Rover trips to Beni, where two young German women and their lady porter were already waiting. On the wall of the house was plastered a faded red poster depicting a cartoon of a kid on crutches and another in a wheel chair, ominously overshadowed by images of hypodermic needle cartoon characters with mean faces and a condom with a happy face. The text was written in Nepali, so I couldn't understand the message. The only part of the poster in Roman characters said something about the Elton John Aids Foundation and another organization for the handicapped. From what I could make of it, it looked like a warning to handicapped children threatened by HIV and AIDS through hypodermic drug use and sexual activity. I was in no way educated about the HIV problems in Nepal, but after our walk in paradise, it seemed somewhat out of place. Not only that, but so many problems were crammed into that one poster that it almost seemed unreal. It was unfortunate enough to be handicapped, but handicapped and sexually active with HIV? Hooked on hypodermic drugs? It all seemed a bit too much. Sir Elton John's vision of the world projected on some villagers? Another NGO with a supply-side economics model? Apparently, there was more to this story than met the eye on the trek, and whatever the case, I was impressed, if not slightly amused that Rocket Man's reach went as far as the small house in Nepal.

Paras and Niraj procured our tickets while Nora and I said hello to the German girls. They scoffed at us and quipped the minimum required "Hello" back, with little more interest in speaking with us, but our trucks would not be available for at least half an hour, and with little else to do, we attempted to speak to them again.

"So, where are you from?" we asked after noticing their accents.

"We are from Germany," they said while looking away at some pretend point in the distance and again offering only minimal response.

"From where?" we prodded.

"Cologne," they quipped back.

"What are you doing here?" Nora asked in German, at which they were only slightly interested.

"We are hiking in the hills after working on an NGO project at a river dam," one of the girls replied. "I had a project here for school working at the dam, but it was very tiresome and the people are totally clueless. I had a little time to myself before leaving, so we decided to explore a bit." The arrogance they both projected was shameful. It was as if Nepal was graced by their presence and undergraduate technical know-how. Their young, female porter sat away from them and they had nothing to do with her at all. Their porter was a well-dressed young lady in modern trekking gear and very polite. Something about the girls' cold, unfriendly manner bothered me, as does snobbery in general. How could you come to a country, complain about their people, talk down to them, and then bask in its splendor? I have always thought that quite narrow-minded. The people are as much a part of the land as the mountains, and to label them and distance yourself from your hosts, in my mind, is narcissistic. This "I am alone in this world and the world is mine to enjoy" attitude overflows among some backpackers.

Yes, I was revolted by our German companions, but my comical mind soon kicked in, and I imagined the two girls as characters in the Mike Meyer's *Saturday Night Live* skit, "Sprockets," where sullen, robot-like Germans in black leotards apathetically discuss all things in their insufficient, fatally flawed, postmodern world before machinating wildly to industrial techno music. "Heidi, Nepal's shortcomings are ultimately incurable," one would say in a robot-like German voice.

"Ja, ze are far inferior," Heidi may reply. "Deutschland is far supeeerior." Of course, Germans are some of the friendliest, most rational and honest people I know, and who generally do not find false security in snobbery. The two girls were an exception.

Breaking my daydreaming was the arrival of our white Land Rover, with its smiling passengers. It was the first motor vehicle we had seen in a while as past the village there were no more roads, only foot trails or smaller roads serviced by vehicles that were presumably helicoptered in.

When I say that our vehicle was a Land Rover, I use the term loosely. It only resembled the legendary road vehicle in form. Like the bootleg CDs and North Face gear, the truck that stood before us looked like an imposter. *Do they bootleg trucks here, too?* I wondered. It may have been a Tata version of the Range Rover, welded and wired together from sheets of scrap metal and aluminum. It literally looked like a homemade truck with rusted leaf springs and vacant holes where rivets once kept presumably important components safely bound together. In its own way, though, the truck was a marvel. It was a testament to the resourcefulness of the Nepali people. If they could not afford to buy the latest, overpriced Land Rover, they simply cannibalized several vehicles and engineered them into a single utility vehicle. It might be less attractive, but it could traverse the Himalayan terrain just as well as its genetically superior cousin cruising the streets of suburbia, picking up organic groceries and kids from soccer practice in the West.

A local family making the trip with us showed up for the ride, too: a young girl an older woman, and man. They had several large bags with them and passed them up to the driver to stow on the roof along with our things. By the time everything was stowed, there was an impossibly massive mound of luggage on the roof. At the slightest movement, the chassis teetered precariously, creaking and popping, warning passengers not to board the overburdened steel, sickly elephant. Despite the load, Niraj and Paras perched themselves like nesting eagles atop the luggage and settled in for the ride. Nora and I climbed inside the canvass-covered passenger cab with the Germans, their porter, and the family.

The engine sputtered to life, and the vehicle lurched forward while bouncing side to side as if it were driving atop a huge waterbed. The passenger space was dark and full of dust. The Nepali mother put her arm lovingly around her daughter and held her close. Through the windows in the canvass, I could see the Kali Gandaki down a steep embankment we skirted while teetering, top heavy. One wrong move and we would have careened into the gorge and died in one of those tragic accidents mentioned every so often in the news: "Bus falls into ravine in India killing 30 people." But, there was no use worrying about it. My fate was in God's hands (and the driver's), and if the truck was as old as it looked, then it had been doing this for years.

The constant rocking and jarring bumps were not unusual, but our Nepali passengers seemed unadjusted to it. I looked over at the little girl just in time to see her vomit on herself. The vehicle's movement was too much. Her mom then grabbed the knit cap from her daughter's head and quickly held it to the girl's mouth to collect the vomit. The girl choked some more vomit into the hat, which began to seep through the knitting. A slight stench arose in the cabin and caused a chain reaction of sickness.

The mother and father both began to vomit along with their daughter, trying to put their mouths to the windows in the canvass. They were visibly embarrassed and scrambling desperately to find some solution. Nora and I looked around for some kind of bag, but to no avail. We looked on compassionately and tried to ignore the growing stench, lest we also become sick. Finally, the driver passed back some plastic bags. I wondered if simply riding in a motor vehicle was so uncommon for them that the jarring and swaying was too much for them to stomach, like sea sickness to a landlubber. Fortunately for all of us, we soon reached a small trading town.

After being in the bush for so many days, it felt strange to be returning to civilization. Even though what we were encountering was tiny in comparison to Pokhara and Kathmandu, there was no mistaking it. We were reentering the mainstream with shops full of souvenirs and cigarette ads painted colorfully and surprisingly well on the facades of shops made of cinderblocks. Deep ravines separated the first village we passed through in a way that divided it into three parts, each connected with a steel cable bridge. It looked like something out of *Lord of the Rings*. The sounds of water rushing, the glow of the orange walls of the narrow ravines, the lush green patches blended with grey stone – it was very earthy, very organic, more alive than the arid heights we'd experienced in the previous days.

We trudged our way across a suspension bridge as roosters waited on the other side to greet us. Below, water violently gushed across massive boulders, as the bridge bounced like a trampoline. We entered the small alleyways of the village while men worked on their motorbikes with improvised tools and kids peeked at us from the doorways. They had seen people like us thousands of times by now. On the broader parts of the road, women laid grass mats in the sunlight covered in beans and colorful peppers drying in the sun. I tiptoed over mounds of brown lentils hoping not to offend the on-looking women.

From the small village, we would need to get to Beni, where a bus would take us back to Pokhara. The only way to get there was on a small bus wobbling along a one-way dirt road above a 100-foot sheer drop off. As we reached deeper into civilization, our modes of transportation were slowly improving with each village. We went from a homemade Range Rover to an omnibus with rows of seats placed so close together that you had to sit sideways to prevent your knees from reaching your chin. Our dusty bus teetered down the dirt road towards Beni with a sputtering growl and only inches to spare to a cliff. I was reassured when I couldn't spot any crushed bus carcasses in the ravine below. Driving may be dangerous here, but it seems they drive dangerously safely. I suppose that is necessary in a country without guardrails, reflectors, or street signs.

We arrived at another small village just on the other side of Beni, secured our bags, and walked across a long steel suspension bridge toward the bustling town. Below us, I spotted a mongoose prowling quickly along the riverside. Beni was almost predictably hectic with bus ticket hawkers and vendors frantically converging on us –

each desperate to make some money by proving to be the most annoying and persistent. The tactic must work. Probably half of the tourists brush them off, and the other half, perhaps sensing the urgency of the moment, somehow feel obligated to do business with one of them. By now, we were used to this maniac marketing plan. While I wasn't bothered much by the candy bars, tickets, and toboggans being forced in my face, Niraj quickly boomed authoritatively at the gang of men and told them to cut it out. I was amazed at how they immediately disengaged our group without any hard feelings and bowed their heads a bit – instantly honing in on the next group of westerners.

Smells were slowly coming back to me. Burning trash, deep-fried meats, and vegetables wafted through the air, and the sweet smell of incense mixed with diesel exhaust, filled my crusty nostrils. Unlike the putrid smells of Baghdad, which the diesel, trash, and dung smells reminded me of, the Nepali air did not leave me feeling sick and tainted. Somehow it smelled exotic, full of spice, perfumed with a hint of decay.

Beni's streets *were* chaotic, though. Porters gathered provisions for the uphill trek, pilgrims lined the streets, and the few bewildered tourists flowed unconfidently with the tide of people. Niraj and Paras went straight to a counter after asking a child where they could get bus tickets to Pokara. I looked through the throng of people and saw a large bus parked in front of a row of kiosks. It was finally our turn to ride in an authentic Nepali Tata bus.

The bus was massive – built like a barn on wheels. The magic bus that would take us to Pokhara seemed like a hybrid between a Greyhound coach and a Mardi Gras float. Earlier, we had seen these buses absolutely jam-packed with villagers traveling between Kathmandu and the countryside – arms pinned above heads, faces gasping for air, butts in other people's faces; their faces not bothered by the disorder, but their gazes fixed as if on something distant. They seemingly tolerated the cattle cars by mentally detaching themselves from it. I wondered if we awaited a similar travel experience in the rusting, technicolor elephant of steel. I could hardly wait.

With a few minutes until departure, we had time to buy some traditional Nepali snacks like Coca-Cola, Lay's potato chips, and Snickers. I opted for an ice-cold Miranda orange soda and some ketchup flavored chips – a decidedly toxic mix, but at that moment it was better to eat and drink something sterile for the sake of my recovering bowels. Had I known what awaited us, I would have opted not to eat or drink anything whatsoever.

Nora and I boarded the bus and stashed our junk food in the overhead rack. I went atop the bus, helping load rucksacks along with Niraj, Paras, and a band of young, French hippies – one of whom had a small child and could speak fluent Nepali, according to Niraj. For the hippies, rooftop seating wasn't just an unconventional perspective. It was the official dope- smoking section. I secretly conspired to ride atop the bus in true Nepali fashion at some point, even if it meant creeping out of the window while Nora slept.

The two German tourists passed their bags up to us. We strained to get them topside because of their incredible weight – like potato sacks full of rocks! I thought for a moment about the Nepali girl porter who was carrying their bags for them, and how she could have possibly carried such weight for so long. A Marine would have struggled with that load. She seemed dignified, friendly, and professional though. I noticed how she arranged the tickets for the Germans, brought her things onto the bus in a seat next to ours, and then went to the toilet house nearby. Her work was almost done for this particular trip – and she had worked hard for her pay.

Preparing to depart Beni was something like preparing the space shuttle for launch. Rooftop riders get snuggled into their seats, the engine roars to life, and all eyes focus on the steel elephant about to limp out of town. Vendors frantically ran alongside the bus selling roasted chickpeas, struggling to pass goods up and collect the money coming down. Through a large hole in the floor near my foot I could see the tread, or lack of tread, on the rear tires.

Just before leaving, a lanky boy paced the aisle of the bus with the sharp eye of a hustling businessman. His little brown face possessed the gravitas of an old man. His posture was that of a confident manager. His voice was high-pitched and commanding. Up and down the aisle he walked with an impressive wad of cash in his hand. Like a bookie, he collected fares, instantly licked his thumb, and dealt out change in a flash. He inspected our ticket with a critical eye, huffed with approval, and then went on to the others.

By now the bus was rumbling, rattling, and diesel exhaust was leaking into the passenger area through rust holes in the floor. Little Humphrey Bogart went to the front of the bus and leapt out onto the dirt square. Just as the bus was pulling out, Niraj mentioned that the girls' porter had not returned from the toilet yet. When we asked the two about it, one responded with an air of cold indifference that "we can go ahead and leave her. She's late." I was disgusted. The porter's bags were on the bus, she had brought the two brats and their over packed bags across very challenging terrain, and now they were just going to leave her behind like a used donkey? Luckily, Niraj and Paras had been talking to the porter since we made it to the first vehicle stop and were careful not to let the bus leave without her. The girls looked on arrogantly, without remorse. It outraged me, but at the same time I was thankful Niraj and Paras were paying attention. A few seconds later the Nepali girl ran to the bus with a grin.

Little Bogart ran around the bus to guide the driver, slapping the sides of the steel elephant with a loud *WHACK!* whenever we came close to an obstacle, as if a brush with a wall would have damaged the bus any more. He ran about like a soldier before jumping back on the bus and standing sentry at the broken boarding door. If anyone wanted to board the bus, they would have to deal with him first. With a metallic growl like a tractor out of gear, our metal box lurched forward and out of the town square with vendors clinging to the sides making frantic, last second exchanges of fried chickpeas for cash.

A trip that would have taken about an hour on a highway in the West took what seemed like forever. Squeaking and clanking like a rusty panzer, we rocked along a gravel road with the tires only a foot away from a sheer drop off. The view from my window across the valley was more like a window seat in an airplane, but the hole in the floorboard reminded me that there was precious little soil under the tires, and very little room for error. The bus driver was unfazed though, dividing his attention equally between watching the road and carrying on a heated conversation with little Bogart. As with so many other times in these situations, I simply surrendered to the fact that my life was in someone else's hands. But heights were the least of our worries.

The novelty of the bus ride soon wore off when it became clear there were no shocks on the beast. It was bad enough to feel like we were sitting in a Radio Flyer wagon endlessly being pulled across railroad ties, but the parasite didn't seem to agree with the abuse either. With my bowels in code red, I quickly realized the sheer stupidity of eating ketchup-flavored potato chips awash in orange soda. Like a baking soda and lemon juice elementary school science fair experiment, my stomach was erupting and nature was calling. No, it was screaming.

After an hour of sitting atop the pile driver on wheels, the road improved, winding and following the contour lines of the hills. Luxuries like tunnels, highway bridges, and viaducts that slash transit times from A to B to a fraction of time remained a dream. On this trip of about 40 miles (about 60 kilometers), we were going from point A to Z and making all the intermediate stops. But, there is also some beauty in taking the long way home. We passed monkeys perched roadside, colorful villages, and terraced farmland being plowed by nothing but skinny men waist-deep in mud steering wooden plows behind water buffalo. We passed throngs of people gathered hillside to hear politicians speak in a carnival-like atmosphere. And speaking of carnival-like atmosphere, I noticed a funny trend in many villages we passed through.

Alcohol advertisements seem to have a universal format: babes and cash money, good times. Nepal is no different, but the juxtaposition of austere villages and a Ken doll-like westerner cruising in a boat stocked full of whiskey and bikini-clad young ladies was surreal. No, it was a vision of heaven for some men here. The knockoff whiskey brand was probably doing more to promote western culture with its ads than the entire public affairs section at the U.S. embassy in Kathmandu.

A different ad appealed to Nepali themes instead of south Florida ones. It featured a strong-looking Nepali man tethered to a high-tension power line tower, inspecting it carefully with an amber sunset backdrop. This probably connects at some level with people who live at the top of the world and have a proud heritage of mountaineering. How it connects to whiskey, I'm not sure, because hanging out in a spider web of high voltage wires with double vision at sunset seems like an experience to die for. So whether it's the Swedish Bikini Team in American commercials pushing watery headache juice, or a whisky company selling bravado with scenes worthy of several workplace safety citations, it would seem that alcohol is the universal escape for east and west, rich and poor. No matter what the budget, or how depressed an economy, there always seems to be spare change laying around for booze and smokes. Hey – a man's gotta live!

After the longest 40 miles I have ever traveled, our bus barreled into Pokhara city limits. We pulled into what could loosely be called a gas station. Many of these rudimentary stations featured hand-painted Castrol and other logos. This artwork, found across the country, may not seem like anything special, but the more I saw it, the more I realized it required a lot of skill. Some of these paintings were marketing masterpieces, and had a certain charm our uniform plastic signage in the West lacked. Of course, they also took much longer to produce and didn't have any fussy branding or franchise permissions. Nonetheless, you had to respect whoever was painting the murals for being the very best at what they were doing. Pondering Nepali gas station art, I watched little Bogart flip through a wad of cash while chatting up the pump attendant. The attendant took a funnel and poured thick motor oil down the gas tank before filling it up with diesel from a dilapidated pump. His oil-soaked clothes and calloused, oil-stained hands made me wonder if he would spontaneously combust at any moment. All around was a circus-like churn of people on mopeds, feral dogs running the streets, children playing with plastic bottles, and cows sitting in the middle of rushing traffic. The scene was at once depressing and exhilarating. These streets were alive.

Our last night in Pokhara was much better than our first. The guys found us a comfortable hotel in town, and we went out for a victory dinner at a local tourist dive on the lake. The entire country was struck with cricket fever, with tourists and locals blending at a big screen going absolutely berserk at men in sweater vests and something called wickets. Some drunken middle-aged Brits hung on each other while singing Bob Marley songs. We all sat under the light of the full moon and tiki torches sipping Everest beer and eating pizza. Paras and Niraj were clearly fired up from the trip and wanted to celebrate, but Nora and I were party poopers. I've been known to party hard, but on that night, the Everest beer was filling and bitter, and I was caught between reflecting on the serenity of the trip and reentering civilization. Not only that, but the now-tamed parasite had sucked the energy out of me. While somewhere deep inside I was envious of the Bob Marley singers and wanted to go off to Margaritaville and dance on a bamboo table, I was exhausted and buoyed in some kind of monastic, aesthetic state of mind. I was ready for sackcloth and ashes, not Red Bull and vodka. After some good conversation, Nora and I excused ourselves for the evening so Paras and Niraj could prowl the town properly. From the looks of them the next morning, they accomplished that mission grandly. They earned it.

pokhara to kathmandu

U nlike the Tata beast that brought us from Beni to Pokhara, we returned to Kathmandu in a so-called "VIP" bus. It seemed sterile and soulless compared to the local buses careening past us with people perched on top, wind blowing through their hair. We wound along the Kali Gandaki and Trishuli river valleys for hours. With my head against the glass, I watched the serene waters dance across the wide basin making its way slowly to the sacred Ganges River in India. The glacial Himalayan waters passed through here as they had for millennia. My moment in time in Nepal was but a nanosecond or less in the great history of Earth. It reminded me of my own mortality, the awesomeness of our planet, and the mysteries surrounding it.

Taking mental pictures of families working fields with their bare hands, villages, and towering peaks, I thought about the passing of time. Savoring every second, each turn in the road, every smile shared with a passenger packed like a sardine in buses overtaking us with their melodic horns. Time passed like sand through my fingers, like water over the rocks in the valley. I was enjoying the moment and reminding myself that this would all be a memory soon. The intense burst of creativity and child-like wonder, an elusive state of mind traveling always unlocked for me, would soon be numbed by my daily routine back home.

But, routines are needed. A successful routine made this trip possible. I couldn't bring myself to throw all caution to the wind like the French hippies in Beni. I couldn't turn on, tune in, drop out in some ganga haze and wander the earth like a Sadhu. Everything in moderation, adventure and work, the kind of work that made sure Nora and I could one day have kids, a house of our own, and a good retirement. We weren't going to live completely for tomorrow, but we weren't going to simply live for today either. The answer for us was somewhere in-between. Suddenly, I realized that was another lesson of this trip. It's not the routine that becomes depressing but whether or not it's balanced. On these trails, we often met the adventure addict, the person without a routine. That lifestyle seemed gratifying for them personally, but in conversations with them, one also seemed to feel they had to keep looking for the next high. It was a restlessness that could quickly make its master its slave. White sandy beaches or Himalayan trails are pure fantasy for many. Being able to enjoy them for just a few days, or even weeks, offers a taste of something exotic without setting those seedling roots too deep. A dream becomes reality, but not for long enough to become familiar. In not becoming familiar, fantasy fills in the gaps, leaves us wondering and wanting to return to recapture that moment. It adds an extra vibrancy to the experience and memories. So, in a way, I should be thanking my routine, I thought. Without it, those brushes with fantasy would seem less magical.

Our bus finally descended into Kathmandu Valley in the early evening and was immediately swallowed up by traffic, people, and animals. Like a lava flow, we all crept at a snail's pace through the densely packed streets. The contrast between the Mustang and the bustling metropolis was extreme, and at first overwhelming, like a shock of ice water to the face. Getting nowhere, we decided to dismount the bus and make our way on foot through the crush of people until we found a taxi that could bring us back to Krishna's house. We quietly rode together, decompressing from the trip in our own way.

"Now you have seen the real Nepal!" Krishna said when we arrived at the house. "I wish I could go with you!"

"It was amazing," I said. "The most amazing trip I have ever made. This country is beautiful."

Krishna and the family were happy to see that we made it back in good spirits. "Yes, I heard you are very sick. You may need to go see the doctor?"

"I think I'll be okay. It's under control now. I'll see a doctor when I get back to Germany."

"I think from what I've heard, you have giardia, man," Jenash said. He would know as a medical student. "Look, you already lost a lot of weight!" He was right. I probably dropped 10 pounds since he saw me last.

"Yes, you need some rest tonight. No partying. Relax and gain your strength back. Jenash will bring you some more medicine," Krishna said. "We'll make you some tea."

We unloaded our bags and decided to go out for a victory dinner at a local restaurant overlooking the city. Paras, Niraj, Jenash, and some other friends joined us for dinner. There was no milky rice beer or raw water buffalo meat. I took some French fries and Coca-Cola, a pretty safe bet. I was less interested in food and more in the people sitting at the table. They were my age, young, and smart. Most of them studied at university. Many of them had dreams they wanted to realize in Nepal, not as expats in a foreign country. They could easily leave the country for more money elsewhere, but the bond to their country, even if it was imperfect, was too strong to break. Everyone at the table had a vision for a better Nepal and a better future. They didn't simply wish for it, they were actively working to achieve it. I had a feeling that these people would shape the future of Nepal at some point, in government or other institutions.

After a long night of trading stories about tomato girl and other adventures, we decided it was time to head home for the night and say goodbye to our new friends. It was the last time we would see Niraj and Paras. They made our trip possible. They taught us so much about Nepal and its culture. We never discovered the snow leopard, but we did forge a friendship that has continued ever since.

We were sad to be leaving Nepal but ready to return home. On our last morning, Nora and I sat on Krishna's roof overlooking the orange haze across Kathmandu Valley while I wrote in my journal about the past days on the Annapurna Circuit, the incredible hospitality we encountered, and the rich culture we came to love. Below, kids waved to us from balconies and played peek-a-boo. Before leaving for the airport, Krishna gathered the family along with us for a group photo. It was surreal. What began as a conversation back in Germany a few years earlier became reality in that moment. We crossed the globe to make this moment happen. Nora and I would be forever grateful for the experience they'd given us, despite their busy schedules. Triza presented Nora with a shalwar kameez and Jenash gave us a wooden carving before we left. We were flattered, but the truth was, they didn't need to give us anything. If anything, we owed them. They gave us a beautiful gift: a home away from home.

"We really appreciate this, but it's not necessary," I said.

"Dan, this is something from Nepal to remember us by," Krishna said. "Take this back with you and tell other people about Nepal and its hospitality."

"We are going to miss you all. I have a feeling this won't be the last time we see each other." I said with as little emotion as possible. It was a way of coping with meeting so many interesting people and then having to say goodbye just as I was becoming good friends with them. In this case, I knew there must have been a customary goodbye, and I knew I should have learned it by then, but I had to hug Krishna and the family. It was as much to say goodbye as it was to reaffirm that the moment was real. The entire trip felt like a dream, even to the point where I wasn't totally sure whether I was dreaming or not on some mornings. This place, one that had fascinated me since picking up a

National Geographic Magazine when I was a kid, was no longer a mystery. It was no longer an exotic destination for only the privileged or retirees. It wasn't a check on a list. It was a community held together by common interests, and dreams much like those in other places we visited. People who wanted a better future for their children and a good quality of life – people who wanted access to good work and honest pay, and the opportunity to make a difference. Nepal was part of us now and would shape our ideas about the world around us for the rest of our lives. Sitting in the departure hall, about to board our flight to Doha, I thought about the sign I first read when we landed in Nepal. It read "Nepal is not here for you. It is not here for you to change. It is here to change you."

13

the homecoming

Doha International Airport in Qatar was sparkling, but I was not looking forward to returning there for the connecting flight to Frankfurt. It seemed like a black hole that could suck you in and spit you out with style – and hours delayed. Sure enough, as we arrived in Doha from Kathmandu, we learned that our flight would be delayed an hour or two. We weren't alone, though. Throughout the gleaming white terminal stranded travelers ranging from French backpackers to Pashtun elders lay unconscious on the cold marble floors and in hidden corners. Nothing here seemed to run on time.

In some ways, the Doha airport was a symbol of progress in the Middle East – all form and no substance. Intercoms designed to inform passengers about their delayed flights weren't the slightest bit intelligible even at close range as they echoed in the large hall. But they were there, and that is all that mattered. High-tech flat panel screens filled the terminal with the latest flight information, blinking with delay notices. Even these were inaccurate as the gates listed for flights didn't correspond with the proper aircraft. In trying to catch a flight to Delhi, you may go to gate 23 as listed on the screen, only to find out that it is actually departing out of gate eight. Or, as was our case, you could read that the flight to Frankfurt was out of gate 20, see a line at gate 20, only to realize that the line for gate 20 was for a flight to London, that the

Frankfurt flight gate was moved downstairs to gate five 20 minutes ago, and that you were about to miss your flight. But, all that mattered was that the Qatar airport had high-tech screens. Never mind that they didn't function and sometimes didn't even list all of the flights. In Doha, you play musical boarding gates, and I had a feeling that the loser misses their flight.

I was relieved when we finally dog-piled into a bus despite the Germans with their bristling, stiff elbows jabbing me. I tried not to think about returning to Germany where I had become used to shameless, *every man for himself* trampling in lines. After what seemed like forever driving across a vast desert tarmac in the dark, we pulled alongside our aircraft and boarded. The dry desert wind reminded me of when I left Kuwait for home after more than a year in Iraq. Nora and I settled into our seats, and I realized that a young American officer was sitting next to me. I gathered he was not in the mood for conversation with American civilians, as he quickly buried his nose in a novel. With the war in Iraq raging and Afghanistan picking up, the man's fate was still tightly wound around a conflict that I had long since parted ways with. I thought about the sharp contrast between my visit to Qatar in 2004 and that evening, how much things had changed for me, how I could have very well been that young man sitting on the plane years later if I hadn't decided to leave the Army for good. While I respected his service, and fully supported the troop surge in Iraq in a last-ditch effort to make a difference there, I reflected on how I was now in charge of my life. I decided where I was going to go and spend my time, my resources. The time in Nepal made me wiser. It introduced me to inspirational people who wanted to make a difference in their country and make it better. I had done my time for my country, gone where it told me to go, fought the war it thought was critical to our national security. Now, I would be deciding what was important to me, how I could best contribute my talents, be it in public or private service.

An hour later we took flight into the warm gulf air. During the first meal service, two stewardesses became visibly angry with each other and began shouting. I didn't catch what the problem was, but one stewardess refused to serve and immediately went to the back of the plane in protest. I had never seen anything like it before. The airline employs many expatriates who are not Qatari. Many are western and Asian – Thai and Filipino – so maybe there is some clash of cultures within an airline that has to employ foreigners to run their operation. After all, I didn't see any Arab women at work.

We landed in Frankfurt early on a crisp, sunny and beautiful morning. As we exited the plane, I noticed a man holding a small digital camcorder filming two men in front of me. He was following them and seemed to be part of their group. As I passed, one of them looked at me and I shot him an amused grin. It was Tom Arnold – former husband of Rosanne Barr and host of the popular ESPN *The Best Damn Sports Show Period*. Walking alongside him was a younger man wearing a desert camouflage blouse, whom I later found out was actor Dax Shepard. I was able to follow their conversation as Shepard said, "You know, I was totally against the war…and I still am. But you know, after seeing those guys down there, you can't help but feel patriotic. You can really feel it." I later googled "Tom Arnold" and "Qatar" and found that Arnold and Shepard were on a United Service Organizations (USO) entertainment tour for the troops throughout the Middle East.

"Nora, that's Tom Arnold," I said, almost embarrassed that I was raising it to her attention. I hardly even knew about Tom Arnold, but thought it was funny he was on our flight.

"Who's Tom Arnold?" was Nora's uninterested reply. And who could blame her? Why would a German girl know who Tom Arnold is? I was still somewhat fascinated with this brush with petty celebrity.

"You know, he was married to that comedian Rosanne Barr?" I explained, as if Nora would know who Rosanne Barr is.

"Who's Roxanne Barr?" she asked.

"Rosanne Barr. Ah, it's a long story," I said, realizing that Nora was deprived of the minor details of American television culture that even I had only absorbed tiny shreds of before coming to Germany when I was 18. How could two people – one knowing of Tom Arnold and the other not – *possibly* fall in love and overcome these serious culture gaps? I'm not sure, but somehow we managed. I realized that bothering Nora about Tom Arnold wasn't worth her time, and was almost embarrassed I'd even mentioned it.

Nora's mom Biggy was kind enough to pick us up at the airport. Nora and I both got the impression our parents were not thrilled that we'd developed an interest in traveling to politically unstable parts of the world. As we walked into the arrivals hall, Nora's mom beamed and gave us a hardy embrace. We made it back alive!

Despite the encroaching anxiety of returning to our routine life, it was good to be back in Frankfurt. We craved Biggy's famous homemade Frankfurt Green Sauce, a meal of boiled potatoes and eggs smothered in a zesty herb and yogurt sauce. After eating curry for over two weeks straight, we smelled like an Indian kitchen. Our pores pumped out cumin, cardamom, turmeric, and garlic vapor. I was oblivious to it, but a few days later standing in line at a store, a woman asked her friend, "Do you smell that? It smells really strong like curry." Hmmm. I wonder where that was coming from? Maybe it was time to change my diet for a while.

As we left Frankfurt airport and merged onto the Autobahn leading to the city center and our apartment, the contrast between Germany and Nepal began to hit me. The airport alone was a culture shock. Frankfurt International Airport looked like a space station compared to the Kathmandu airport. The autobahns were meticulously maintained compared to the roads in Nepal. German traffic signs were labeled with exact precision, even framed with custom poles for maximum *Germaness* – a category of unforgiving exactness, utility, and efficiency – unlike the faded and rusted signs we saw in Nepal. Guardrails lined roads, sidewalks consisted of intricate masonry, and nearly every vehicle on the road was relatively new. Everything radiated extreme order and safety. If it weren't so desirable, it would almost seem militant. This contrast between highly developed Germany, where the amount of labor and resources put into a common street sign would probably be unthinkable for most economies, and that of poor Nepal, was simply striking, especially in regards to safety precautions. In the West, we're surrounded by a virtual safety net when we drive, eat, and work. Little things like guardrails and airbags are part of our lives, whereas buses falling into ravines and planting one's face in a hard steering wheel is a reality for some in Nepal. In Germany, cameras take your photo if you run a traffic light and an automated system will ensure you get ticketed within days. In Nepal, few obey the traffic lights, and still fewer could afford to pay the fine anyways. But for a fleeting moment, as ultra-modern Germany went past my passenger window, I missed Nepal and its disorder.

"G-L-A-M-O-R-O-U-S" was being spelled out word for word on the radio in a little diddy by Black Eyed Peas member Fergie, conjuring images of Louis Vutton, sippin' on Champaign while flying first class – and, well, being glamorous. With images of poor, yet happy villagers still fresh in my mind, I couldn't help but see some tragedy in some of our western culture. The song's refrain, in an aggressive and boisterous African-American voice, chanted "If you don't have no money, take yo broke ass home!" I thought about all the "broke ass" people I was just with and thought to myself that being poor or broke or not being able to sip Cristal on a private jet doesn't make you any less of a person. Without trying to get too cerebral or maudlin about it, some of the western culture and the messages our pop culture carries – money is happiness, women are objects, and pleasure is all that matters – were already annoying me. As the award-winning "Glamorous" ballad and later "My Humps" played on the radio, I couldn't help but miss the bustling streets of Kathmandu, the Buddhist chants wafting through the morning air of Pokhara, or the simple happiness of those we met along our journey. Although I shouldn't have felt like it, the initial culture shock of being back in Europe made me feel like a pilgrim in an unholy land.

I returned to work on Monday with a positive attitude. I entered the hallway and our graphic designer was shocked.

"Oh my God, you look like you just got back from fat camp!"

"What do you mean?"

"I mean you lost a lot of weight!"

"I want to lose that much weight!" another coworker said.

"Oh yeah, that! I have some kind of parasite. I think it's called giardia. Some kind of amoebic dysentery from eating bad food in Nepal." My stomach was still gargling loudly and would continue for at least a month.

"Damn! You need to find a way to bottle that up! I wouldn't mind having a little giardia if it works that good!"

"Yeah, you may be on to something, but I think you can just eat dog poop and get the same results. It's common in stray dogs and outside pets," I laughed.

It was good to be back with my marketing team, good friends. But, when I turned on my computer, hundreds of e-mails from the past weeks poured in. Post vacation depression was kicking in. But somehow, this was heavier than usual. This was more depressing than settling back in the office after a beach vacation in Turkey. This was coming back to civilization after a life changing experience. I took a deep breath, put my head in my hands, and took a long pause. My joyful return from the Himalayas quickly gave way to about as much enthusiasm for my job as someone going in for a colonoscopy.

We had dreamed of going east and exploring the Himalayas. It was a dream that for many remains out of reach, or only something to be experienced on the Travel Channel. Nora and I made it come true. We set a goal and reached it. Most of all, I learned what for others was an obvious fact of life: we *do* have the power to make our dreams come true. I was used to living my life as a soldier coming from a rather structured household. I wasn't used to taking big risks and setting my own agenda. For me, going from asking for permission to do things to dreaming and charting a course to achieve them was a major life event. Going to Nepal changed how I have dealt with life ever since. It also deepened an insatiable hunger to explore the planet, to sit on shop floors with people and discuss hopes and dreams, and to constantly reaffirm that the people of the world are more alike than they are different, no matter what politicians and the media would like us to believe. For me, travel is the discovery of truth; an affirmation of the promise that human kind is far more beautiful than it is flawed. With each trip comes a new optimism that where there is despair and hardship, there are ideas and people just waiting to be energized, to be empowered, to make a difference for good. People power could make a difference if it could be harnessed, if hierarchies could be flattened, if the old power structures that continued to stifle innovation around the world could be circumvented. I wanted to help play a role in that process, perhaps through technology. Perhaps using social media to make governments more transparent, to help villagers share ideas in real time, to facilitate political involvement. Little did I know that this idea of using technology to circumvent power, an idea that came to me while hiking through villages in the Annapurna, would become a tactic used in the 2009 Iranian Green Revolution and wider Arab Spring. It would also become the foundation of my graduate thesis on social media and strategic non-violent conflict. I had the people of Nepal, guys like Paras and Niraj, to thank for opening my mind to these possibilities.

Maybe I also had Muktinath to thank, too. Being Catholic, I believe in the primacy of the Father, Son, and the Holy Spirit. But traveling the world, I am also convinced, as the Church expressed, that there are rays of light from many religions that reflect truth, that nothing that is holy and true should be rejected in other religions. The asceticism of the Sadhu and monk, the Hindu reverence and love for a higher power were all-inspiring during our travel in Nepal. They were kindred spirits, and in some ways, that was one of the great attractions of exploring less developed countries. To borrow from Steve Jobs, they were still hungry for a better future, they were still foolish. They still valued what many of us have long since taken for granted. They didn't find false hope and gratification in indulgences of the ego and mindless consumption. And while these thoughts swirled in my head, and certainly some of them were simply inspired nonsense at the time, I went to check my mailbox.

Inside was a letter with a sizable check and notice that I was diagnosed for deafness related to combat in Iraq and would be retroactively compensated. I would also receive a very small stipend from now on. My hearing was extremely poor following a grenade attack on my convoy in Iraq, and, later, an almost direct improvised explosive device strike on my unarmored Humvee. My hearing problem became extremely annoying, and I had it looked at. I was constantly asking people to repeat themselves and forced to nod when spoken to when really I missed critical parts of what was being said. I learned to compensate by turning my head to whoever was speaking or cupping my hand nonchalantly around my ear if I was sitting.

The Department of Veterans Affairs reviewed my case and granted a very small disability judgment. While I was never one to actively seek out a government handout, it also probably didn't make any sense to pay for my own hearing aid if there was assistance available to Iraq War vets. In any event, the amount of the check pretty much covered a sizable chunk of the trip we just took to Nepal. It was completely unexpected. After all, I only wanted my service-related hearing status officially recorded, not money. As I put the check back in the envelope, I noticed the postmark. It was sent on March 23, 2007 – the same day we reached Muktinath Temple and received a ritual blessing. I could have written this off as simple coincidence, but the lessons of our Nepal trip were still with me. Dreams make life wonderful. Following where those dreams take you is what makes it magical.

acknowledgments

Writing this book was truly a worldwide team effort. I wrote this book in Seoul, Korea and Heidelberg, Germany, not sure if it would ever become a reality. With the help of my family and friends around the globe, it is now in your hands. I owe many thanks to my editorial team, Dr. George Skipworth, Barbara Wester, and J.A. Tyler for many hours rewiring my broken sentence structure and spicing it with proper punctuation.

I owe special thanks to Mike Evans for his sharp eye and encouragement. Thanks to fellow intrepid traveler Jake Watson for connecting me to the right folks to help make this project a success.

I am especially grateful to Dr. Alec McEwen, Professor Emeritus of Geomatics Engineering at the University of Calgary, for his generous, collaborative spirit. His review led to many improvements in the manuscript. While I am simply a tourist, Dr. McEwen is truly advancing geographical science and knowledge. We owe our understanding of the world around us to him and those like him.

For their friendship, advice, and highlighting my earlier writings, I am very thankful to Karl Weisel, Geoffrey Carter, Casey Kugler, Sissy and Dan Caffarel, Sarah and Johannes Stolz, and Shane Goldberg. For their professional mentoring and encouragement, I am indebted to Dr. Deborah Winslow Nutter, Colonel Todd Walsh, Kathleen Marin, Michelle Watts, Robert Myers, and Nicki Sass.

For being a constant source of inspiration and friendship over the past two years, I am humbled by Mark Mullinix, Pablo Rabczuk, Enrique Alanis, Jake Watson, Andrew Gordon, Dr. Akjemal Magtymova, and Dalia Ziada. Never, never, never give up!

I owe so much to my family, biological and adopted. For steadfast support and encouragement, I am grateful to Jimmy Bunn and family; the best in-laws one could imagine, Biggy and Volker; and my parents. I would also like to thank Russ and Kyoung Wicke for their fantastic support in our time of need. A special note of thanks goes to Kai Gebel, a wonderful human being and photographer who helped Nora and me capture beautiful moments with our two newborn sons, Liam and Luis. As this book went to press, Liam Munroe Thompson passed away in my arms six hours after birth. Every breath he took was a gift, and each minute with him was like an hour. Liam truly taught us to appreciate life, and Luis has helped us remember to celebrate it.

Above all else, I am *still* pinching myself each morning that I am married to my best friend and travel buddy, Nora. Without her unconditional love and support, none of this would be possible. I love you to the moon and back.

recipes

dal bhat

ingredients

Plain Rice (Bhat)

2 cups rice (Basmati or Long grain preferred)

4 cups (1 lt) water

1 tsp butter (optional)

Lentils (Dal)

1½ cups lentil (any kind)

4 to 5 cups of water (depends preference of your consistency of liquid)

½ tsp turmeric

1 tsp garlic, minced

6 tbsp clarified butter (ghee)

3/4 cup sliced onions

2 chillies (dried red chilies preferred) (depends on your preference)

Salt to taste

optional

¼ tsp (pinch) asafetida

¼ tsp (pinch) jimbu

1 tbsp fresh ginger paste

preparation

Rice

Wash rice and soak for 5 minutes. Boil the rice over medium heat for about 10 -15 minutes. Stir once thoroughly. Add butter to make rice give it taste as well as make it soft and fluffy.

Turn the heat to low and cook, covered, for 5 more minutes until done.

Lentils

Wash lentils and soak lentil for 10 minutes. Remove anything that float on the surface after it and drain extra water.

Add drained lentils in fresh water and bring to a boil again. Add all spices. Reduce the heat and simmer, covered, for 20 to 30 minutes until lentils are soft and the consistency is similar to that of porridge. In a small pan heat the remaining of butter and fry the onions, chilies and garlic. Stir into the lentils few minutes before you stop boiling. Serve with rice.

Adapted from http://food-nepal.com

nepali milk tea

Nepali Spiced Chiya
(Spiced Tea, Nepali style)

ingredients
1 pouch or 1 tablespoon black tea, Nepali or Indian
1 cup whole milk
1 teaspoon sugar
2 pods green cardamom, bruised
2 cloves
1 pod black cardamom (alaichee), bruised (optional)
1/4 teaspoon freshly ground pepper (optional)
1 teaspoon ginger, chopped
1 small cinnamon stick
Pinch of salt
Cooking Instructions:

In a small cooking pot, pour milk; add all the other ingredients. Set heat to low; bring mixture to a boil and allow simmering for about 5 minutes. Strain tea with a help of a tea strainer. Serve hot.

Adapted from http://www.explorenepal.com

biographies

The Acharya Family includes Triza Acharya, a retired banker, who together with seven other women are working to empower women at all social and economic levels through self-help programs affiliated with the Social Welfare Council of Nepal in association with the Women Skill Development Organization (WOSDO). Krishna Prasad Acharya, a retired director of the Nepal Disabled Association, is currently working as a country representative of Council Of International Fellowship, Nepal (CIF). It is primarily focused on cultural exchange programs worldwide with the objective of sharing the socio-economic values of different countries around the globe. Triza and Krishna are the proud parents of son Dr. Jenash Acharya and daughter Dr. Jemish Acharya, who both besides pursuing their master's degrees in Forensic Medicine and Public Health respectively, help their parents with their post retirement endeavors.

Paras Shrestha is one of the founders of the NGO Tourism Development Endeavors. He is also founder of Ka'si, a Newari-style restaurant. Paras completed his bachelor's degree at the National College Center for Development Studies. Paras is an expert traveler and experienced photographer who has hiked the Mustang District extensively and trekked through almost every part of Nepal in his pursuit to understand culture, document knowledge and promote sustainable tourism destinations.

Since 2004, he is working with Dwarika's hotel. He lives in Kathmandu and can be reached at paras_shr@hotmail.com for travel and consulting inquiries.

Niraj Tamrakar is one of the founders of the NGO Tourism Development Endeavors (TUDE), an organization dedicated to sustainable, ethical and decentralized tourism in Nepal. He is also chairperson of Incredible Holidayz Travel and Tours Nepal and Afnai Products Best Option Events and Marketing Company promoting Nepali crafts and sustainable tour packages. He is a consultant to the Hands-On Institute and Carbon Investigate and Analysis Nepal, while working with International Climate Champions Network Nepal, an NGO working in environment and sustainable development programs. He is a graduate of Kathmandu University, where he mastered in Environmental Education and Sustainable Development (EESD) and published his thesis "Culture and Conservation" in 2012. He has traveled to Australia, India and Bangladesh. He has hiked the Mustang and almost every part of Nepal in his pursuit to understand culture, document knowledge and promote sustainable tourism destinations. He is also a keen photographer who organizes the Places and Faces of Nepal photo exhibition.

Since 2009, he is working with the British Council as an International Climate Champion. His projects are focused on the Rural-Urban Connection program and the Our Mountains, Our Responsibility campaign for conservation and promotion.

He lives in Kathmandu with his family. Niraj can be reached at nirajnt@gmail.com for travel and consulting inquiries.

Nora Thompson is the International Coordinator for the University of Mannheim's Legal Studies Program. She has previously worked with

the Goethe Institut, German Academic Exchange Service (DAAD), and assisted the Korean National Commission for UNESCO while living in Seoul, Korea. She is a graduate of Frankfurt, Germany's Goethe University with a master's degree in Geography and studied abroad at Korea University. Her thesis, "Benefits and Obstacles to Public Engagement in Urban Stream Restoration Projects - A Case Study of the Cheonggyecheon Restoration Project in Seoul, South Korea" was published in 2011 before she was certified as an intercultural trainer at Friedrich-Schiller-University Jena. She has traveled to more than 35 countries and enjoys CrossFit, yoga and is an Indian and Mediterranean food aficionado.

Nora is married to Dan Thompson and lives in Heidelberg, Germany with him and their two sons, Liam and Luis. She can be contacted about intercultural consulting opportunities, especially related to German, American, and Korean culture, at norathompson360@gmail.com.

Dan Thompson served as a combat soldier in Iraq from 2003 through 2004 with the U.S. Army's First Armored Division. Since then, he has served overseas for more than seven years in Asia and Europe in the Unites States Civil Service as a public relations executive. A fellow of the Royal Geographical Society of London and graduate of the Fletcher School of Law and Diplomacy at Tufts University, he was awarded the Superior Civilian Service Award by the United States Army for services rendered in Seoul, South Korea. He now lives in Heidelberg, Germany with his wife Nora and two sons, Liam and Luis. Contact him at danthompson360@gmail.com or follow him on Twitter at @360DanT.

Traditional timbered storefront in downtown Kathmandu selling brass wares.

Jenash and Nora take a break from cruising Kathmandu's streets and alleys.

From left to right: Paras, Niraj, Nora, Jenash, and Dan stand on Patan Durbar Square, a UNESCO World Heritage Site.

Finely chopped water buffalo tartare served with onions.

A man gazes across Patan's Durbar Square from Krishna Temple.

A Nepali woman prepares fried eggs at a traditional
restaurant in Patan.

A Tibetan Buddhist nun walks along a row of prayer wheels at the
Swayambhunath complex.

View of Swayambhunath stupa overlooking Kathmandu Valley. The bronze spire, draped with colorful prayer flags, sits atop a white dome. The stupa complex is known informally as the "Monkey Temple" because of the many monkeys living there.

Two young men take a cruise on Phewa Lake with a local guide in Pokhara.

View from aircraft of Jomsom airport runway shortly after landing. The airfield sits in a deep valley at 8,800 feet (2,682 m).

Dan and Nora stand in front of a Dornier 228 at Jomsom airport. The same type of aircraft crashed there in May 2012 killing 15 of 21 people on board.

Extreme winds blast the Nilgiri Himal range at 23,166 feet (7,061 m) towering over Jomsom.

Dan walks along a sheer rock face early in the day while trekking towards Jharkot.
(Photo by Niraj Tamrakar, copyright 2007. Reprinted with permission.)

Nora and Dan ascend the arid hills towards Jharkot.
(Photo by Niraj Tamrakar, copyright 2007. Reprinted with permission.)

The view north to the Upper Mustang bordering on China and the Tibetan plateau.
Mustang was its own kingdom until 2008.

In a typical configuration, a porter carries a heavy load strapped across his head while
walking along the Kali Gandaki near Jomsom.

Niraj bathes in the holy waters of Muktinath among icicles and snow surrounding the religious site at over 12,000 feet (3710 m).

Gate to Muktinath high in the Himalayas with the peaks of Dhampus (19,520 feet or 5950 m) and Thapa (19,727 feet or 6013 m).

Solar ovens like the one depicted here near Jharkot provide renewable cooking heat and can save up to around 1,000 pounds (about 453 kilos) of wood per month at peak use. (Photo by Niraj Tamrakar, copyright 2007. Reprinted with permission.)

Left to right: Niraj, Nora, and Paras stand atop a cable bridge stretching across the Kali Gandaki gorge.

Two young boys greet passersby with a customary *Namaste* near Lete. The greeting is meant to symbolize bowing to another.
(Photo by Niraj Tamrakar, copyright 2007. Reprinted with permission.)

Paras relaxes next to a lodge fire late at night in Tukche.

Niraj, Paras stand by as Dan shows village children near Lete how he fills his Camelbak with bottled water.

Paras rests along a wall near the town of Lete on the way to Ghasa.

Nora and Dan walk with some schoolchildren outside of Lete on the way to Ghasa.
(Photo by Niraj Tamrakar, copyright 2007. Reprinted with permission.)

Nora takes a nap in the shadow of Nilgiri South before descending to Ghasa.

Women pilgrims make their way uphill
towards Lete in slippers and sandals despite
the treacherous ascent ahead of them.

A typical cable bridge along the Annapurna used by both trekkers and
donkey trains alike. Many of the bridges span dizzying heights.

Road workers with little protection remove rocks by hand along a sheer drop off along the Kali Gandaki.

A Sadhu poses for a photo while on his way to Muktinath from the lowlands.

A trader carries live chickens uphill across rough terrain south of Tatopani.

Dan, Nora, and Niraj relax their tired muscles in Tatopani's hot spring waters.

A typical example of loaded donkey trains competing for space with trekkers.

A ram with a unique horn mutation found south of Tatopani.

A typical Tata bus waiting at a depot in Beni. It would later transport the group back to Pokhara.

The Kathmandu skyline as seen from Krishna's rooftop terrace. When he first built on the property, the skyline was much smaller.

From left to right: Housekeeper, Triza, Nora, Dan, Jenash, and Krishna share one last group photo atop the family home shortly before the conclusion of the visit.

Printed in Great Britain
by Amazon.co.uk, Ltd.,
Marston Gate.